SAVING
BRITAIN'S ART TREASURES

By the same author
Secret Underground Cities
(Leo Cooper, 1998)
Cold War Secret Nuclear Bunkers
(Leo Cooper, 2002)

SAVING BRITAIN'S ART TREASURES

N.J. McCamley

LEO COOPER

First published in Great Britain in 2003 by
LEO COOPER
an imprint of
Pen & Sword Books Ltd
47 Church Street
Barnsley
South Yorkshire
S70 2AS

ISBN 0 85052 918 2

1003093057

A CIP catalogue record for this book is
available from the British Library

Typeset in 10.5/12.5 Plantin by
Pen & Sword Books, Barnsley, South Yorkshire

Printed and bound in England by
CPI UK

CONTENTS

FOREWORD

Thirty-five years ago I worked during my summer holidays from college in a small rubber-processing factory in a village near my home town of Bradford-on-Avon. In those years of full employment holiday jobs were easy to come by and if a factory did not have proper vacancies to fill then jobs would be specially made for students like me. There was ample money available in the company budget for this because wages, in relation to profits, were not high. Being young and interested only in my pay-packet, I was not at first sure what the factory's staple product was. For the first six weeks I worked in the 'rejects' department, a task that involved spending each morning stacking hundreds of sacks containing short lengths of bent rubber tube (all bent to the wrong angle or made the wrong size) on a huge waste heap beside a broad stream that ran through the factory yard. The afternoon summer sun fell squarely upon this waste heap and there, among the sacks of distorted top-hoses and vacuum cleaner tubes, we students, and the odd permanent employee, would doze through the rest of the day until the shift hooter sounded at 5 o'clock. Almost until the end of our first season at the Peradin Rubber Company we all thought the factory actually manufactured 'Rejects' which we believed was a trade name for some esoteric item of flexible automotive hardware. This belief was somewhat reinforced when I was transferred for a short while to the 'Goods Inwards' department and had to unload lorry loads of components from one sub-contractor who consistently, incorrectly and probably maliciously mis-addressed packing cases to 'The Peradin Rubbish Company'. Only later did we come to learn that the company, which had its origins in the manufacture of inflatable decoy tanks and military vehicles during the Second World War, was now a world-leader in the field of rubber-to-metal bonding, making engine mountings and similar items for automotive manufacturers world-wide.

The high rejection rate was due in part to the employment of a great deal of antiquated, obsolescent plant which failed frequently and thus necessitated a disproportionately large staff of maintenance engineers to keep it running. But, as we have seen, labour was cheap so this did not matter. Towards the end of this first summer holiday the maintenance gang was suddenly strengthened by the influx of a batch of third-year apprentices, young local men who were nearing the end of their training, were proficient at their jobs, and who had just been made redundant following the closure of the Royal Enfield motorcycle factory at Westwood, a village a mile or so from the

Peradin plant. The new apprentices told us fantastic stories about their previous place of work. It was, they said, a top-secret underground factory built during the Second World War to manufacture gun-sights and other precision military instruments, but turned over in the post-war years to the building of a range of rather outdated British motorcycles. More fantastic still were their tales of an even more secret area, deep within the quarry beyond their factory, one hundred feet below the ground and sealed by great iron doors. Although a low, background hum of machinery emanated constantly from this secret area, no persons were ever observed passing through the doors except one occasional furtive visitor who spent a few irregular minutes there each month. Local folklore called this secret place 'The Museum', but recollections were hazy about the reason why.

In mid-September I left the factory to resume my college education but returned the following spring to earn a small crust during the long Easter holiday. I was surprised and pleased to find that my employers had taken a short lease on several of the surface buildings associated with the underground factory at Westwood with the intention of using it as temporary storage, and more pleased still to find that my first job was to clear out some of the old and already vandalized offices. In one block the office floors were littered with fragmented plans and drawings, not only of the ill-fated Royal Enfield motorcycles but also of the underground factory itself. The principal building occupied by the rubber company was a former dance-hall and community centre built to provide recreation for the underground workers, for the remote location of the factory and the scarcity of rural public transport in wartime made travelling any distance for amusement virtually impossible. In an idle moment, during one lunchtime, a fellow student-employee and I decided to investigate the dance-hall and the technicalities of its much-vaunted sprung floor. Purely by chance we discovered, concealed behind a large radiator, the end of a three-foot-square concrete duct that dipped slightly into the ground and appeared to run a few feet below ground level out of the building and under the surrounding shrubbery. Burning matches and bits of reject rubber, we decided to investigate further and crawled through the duct for about two hundred yards until we emerged in a large, enclosed concrete chamber. In the floor of this chamber was the open top of a concrete-lined vertical shaft eight feet in diameter and, we were soon to discover, about eighty feet deep. Suspended above the shaft from a beam on the ceiling of the chamber was a large pulley-winch from which hung a forty-gallon oil drum on a stout chain. After a few second's hesitation we climbed into the drum and lowered ourselves down the shaft into the darkness, having no idea what we might be committing ourselves to. Eventually we clanked to a halt in what appeared to be a spacious ante-chamber dimly lit by a few flickering fluorescent tubes. To our right was the inside face of the securely locked great vault door that sealed the mysterious secret inner sanctum from the underground Royal Enfield factory. To our left was a second similar door that concealed, we later learned, one of the greatest and best-kept secrets of the Second World War. Ahead was a third door, partially open, within which a vast air-conditioning and ventilation plant ticked over in standby mode as it had done for the last twenty years, the source of the mysterious hum described by our apprentice engineers. The dirty drum in which we had descended and later made our retreat was used, we discovered, to raise waste boiler-ash from the underground, coal-fired central-heating plant for disposal on the surface and our sub-surface entrance tunnel was a cunning and economic arrangement by which waste heat from the boilerhouse was used to warm the dance-hall.

This, then, was my introduction to Westwood Quarry, the secret underground repository created in 1942, where the nation's priceless treasures from the British Museum, the V&A, and a host of other great national institutions were kept safe from enemy bombardment. We were left in no doubt as to its purpose: inscribed upon the wall in hieroglyphic symbols by Mr C.J. Gadd, the repository's first master and the British Museum's keeper of Egyptian and Assyrian statuary, we found a text which still exists today and in translation reads:

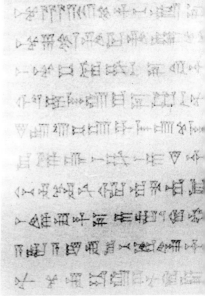

In the year of our Lord 1942
the sixth year of George, King of all lands,
In that year everything precious,
the works of all the craftsmen
which from palaces and temples
were sent out, in order that by fire
or attack by an evil enemy they might not be lost,
into this cave under the earth
a place of security, an abode of peace,
we brought them down and set them.

As thrilling as this discovery was it was, soon

The most important of two hieroglyphic texts inscribed upon the wall of Westwood Quarry by C.J. Gadd, keeper of Egyptian and Assyrian Antiquities at the British Museum.

eclipsed by greater things, for a few months later, our appetites now whetted, my friend and I discovered another disused, wartime underground establishment close by, and this one was of unimaginable proportions. We had found the Monkton Farleigh Central Ammunition Depot, the largest underground ammunition depot in the world, extending over some fifty acres and abandoned by the War Office, despite a capital investment of £4,400,000, in 1966. It was no coincidence that both subterranean sites should be so close. By a quirk of geology the greatest concentration of finest quality oolitic limestone was to be found along the Bath-Corsham axis, and over a period of 200 years dozens of quarries were sunk to exploit these reserves. During the five years before 1939 at least ten of these quarries, vast in extent, deep underground and with a secure overburden of hard rock, were requisitioned by the government for use as munitions stores, armament factories or command centres.

These early discoveries were the spark that initiated a lifetime obsession and an intensive research programme that has spanned four decades. The research culminated in the publication, in 1998, of *Secret Underground Cities*, a history of Britain's wartime underground factories and ammunition depots. Discussion of the art treasures repositories is touched upon in a later chapter of that book, but my investigations had thrown up the existence of yet another huge wartime underground store, - this one for the pictures of the National Gallery – in a disused slate mine at Manod in the Snowdon mountains, and much else besides. To expand upon this material in detail would have resulted in a volume too unwieldy to handle and one that perhaps might never have been completed.

The wartime evacuation of Britain's art treasures was, however, a story that had to be told and I hope that in the pages that follow I have succeeded in unravelling its complexity. At first sight it seemed a straightforward story: I expected the archives to confirm that, on behalf of the great London museums and galleries, the Ministry of Works had planned in the mid-1930s, just like the War Office had done for the Army and its ammunition reserves, to build secure underground repositories for the nation's art treasures in time of war. This, however, was not so although subterranean stores were eventually provided. Faced with popular political antagonism and intense Treasury opposition to further underground construction on grounds of cost, the safety of the nation's cultural treasures was to be assured simply by their evacuation to country houses beyond the immediate boundaries of target 'London'. As the extent of German air raids increased through 1940, more remote accommodation was required but the strategic concept remained the same. But within a year or so of its inception the evacuation scheme fell apart as the self-interest of many, although, to be fair, not all, of the country-house owners who had taken custody of the treasures became increasingly evident. The evacuation was, to a great extent, fatally manipulated by those great landowners seeking, through their wealth, immunity from the effects of war, and by the shabby-genteel, lesser country gentry desperate to hold on to a fading Edwardian dream, who traded off immunity from the compulsory billeting of evacuees or the requisitioning of their property for military purposes in exchange for occupation of a few rooms by the National Gallery or the British Museum. The initial, apparent altruism rapidly degenerated into tension and obstructionism, and was augmented in the Welsh repositories by the fear of an imminent Welsh nationalist uprising. Ultimately, these irreconcilable domestic and nationalistic differences were factors as important as the threat of German bombing in the creation of the central, underground arts repositories in 1941/42.

Throughout my research for this book I have been astonished by the universal and enthusiastic cooperation I have received from everyone I approached for help and advice, from the archivists of the various institutions whose contents were the subject of the great wartime evacuation to the current owners of the quarries and country houses which offered refuge to the evacuated artefacts. In particular I must thank Christopher Date and Garry Thorn, archivists at the British Museum, and to Dudley Hubbard who made such a good job of reproducing, from unpromising contemporary negatives, photographs from the archive there. Thanks, too, go to Christopher Marsden and Martin Durrant at the V&A, and to Andrea Gilbert, archivist of the Wallace Collection, who produced some stunning photographs at exceptionally short notice. I am grateful, too, to Nadaav Soudry for general inspiration and for saving me much time with the translation of Gadd's hieroglyphic text at Westwood Quarry.

Simply compiling a history such as this, which refers to sites so diverse and locations so dramatic, only from documentary evidence runs the risk of sterility, and to avoid this I have endeavoured to visit personally as many as possible in the hope that some of the atmosphere absorbed there might translate into the written word. Of the owners and custodians of these various properties I would like to thank particularly Hugh Taylor of Eastington Hall, which must be the most exquisite country house in England still in private ownership; Nicholas Stephens and the trustees of the Pennington Mellor Charitable Trust, for their kindness at Hellens; Peter Frost-Pennington for providing such excellent photographs of Muncaster Castle; Marian Gwyn for photographs of Penrhyn Castle and Nicola Chandler for providing pictures of Ramster. Thanks, too, are due to Cynthia Webb, Lynn

Kleleman and the Home Farm Trust for allowing me to roam freely around Old Quarries at Avening, the former home of Lord Lee of Fareham, and also for providing some excellent wartime photographs of the house and its contents. I also offer my gratitude to Graham Meaden, the National Trust custodian of Montacute House, and to F.J. Disney, BEM, author of *Shepton Mallet Prison – 380 Years of Prison Regime*, who kindly provided all the photographs and most of the archive material relating to the Public Record Office occupation of the prison.

The former quarry workings and other underground repositories posed their own problems of access and I have to thank Sion Jobbins at the National Library of Wales, Aberystwyth, for photographs of the British Museum tunnel in the library grounds. Several visits to the breathtaking Manod Quarry at Blaenau Ffestiniog in 1986/7 were made easy by Peter Yarbrough, who provided the transport and good company, and by the unnamed quarrymen of Blaenau who allowed us unfettered access to the caverns there. Finally, I must offer a special thanks to Hanson Minerals, and in particular to Zane Swanipole, who organized, against all the odds, a very successful visit to Westwood Quarry in Wiltshire.

INTRODUCTION

Shortly before midnight on Saturday 2 September 1939, to the echo of rolling thunder that marked the end of a long run of hot days and humid nights, the last of six special freight trains slipped out of Camden goods yard in North London. Hauled by the most powerful locomotive the London Midland & Scottish railway could muster, running under the head-code of a Royal Train and with armed guards on the footplate, it sped non-stop through the night on its 240-mile journey, past Birmingham, Stafford, Crewe, Chester and Rhyl to its final destination, the North Wales coastal town of Bangor, in the shadows of the Snowdon range. All along its route lesser trains were held to wait its passing, while at every level-crossing, bridge and tunnel armed police and soldiers stood guard.

Simultaneously, two mysterious road convoys departed from the Capital, one from Kensington, bound for Somerset along the Great West Road, and the other northwards from Bloomsbury into rural Northamptonshire. Meanwhile, two heavily laden lorries with unlikely loads crept out of Bloomsbury and steered towards the London Passenger Transport Board's Lillie Bridge depot to await a late evening ballast train bound for the Aldwych tube.

In the early hours of Sunday 3 September station staff at Bangor, aided by a small detachment of men from Trafalgar Square, began the task of unloading the special night freight. Aboard were 218 paintings, the property of the National Gallery, the most valuable single cargo ever carried on a British railway train and worth, at current valuation, perhaps four billion pounds sterling. This was the last and most valuable batch of some 2,000 pictures hastily evacuated from London and destined to ride out the war deep below ground in disused mine workings in the high, remote and mist-enshrouded mountains above Blaenau Ffestiniog in north-west Wales.

In Somerset, that Sunday, staff from the Victoria and Albert Museum under the guidance of Miss Muriel Clayton, keeper of watercolours, and Mr McDouall, the museum's chief packer, carefully unloaded the lorries. Amongst the day's cargo were the fabulous twelfth century Ardabil carpet, the museum's collection of Dickens manuscripts, over 5,000 watercolours and dozens of items of fifteenth and sixteenth century furniture from the Salting bequest. All this joined many other priceless artefacts that had been arriving at Montacute House every day since 26 August. Less than a year later the shortcomings of Montacute became overwhelmingly apparent and the whole collection was on the move again; forty miles north this time, to the isolated Wiltshire hamlet of Westwood near Bradford on Avon, where it found permanent refuge one hundred feet below ground in a disused stone quarry from where, rather fittingly, stone used in the construction of the South Kensington Museum had been quarried forty years previously.

Earlier that morning the Northamptonshire-bound convoy from Bloomsbury arrived at Boughton House, home of the Duke of Buccleuch. Among its contents were the British Museum's collection of coins and medals, worth, even at 1930s valuation, many millions of pounds. These were dumped unceremoniously on the floor of the Duke of Buccleuch's kitchens where they joined countless other exhibits evacuated in haste from the British Museum. For a while it was thought that Boughton was sufficiently remote from London to be immune from German bombing, but after the fall of France this was no longer so and the Boughton hoard, along with many others, found ultimate refuge alongside the V&A treasures at Westwood Quarry.

Meanwhile, in central London, shortly after the departure of the last passenger service at 11.30 pm on Saturday evening, the Elgin Marbles, which had arrived at Lillie Bridge yard three hours earlier, were manhandled aboard a scheduled maintenance train bound for the Aldwych branch of the Piccadilly line. There, in an abandoned tunnel and firmly crated, they spent the remaining years of the war alongside other Egyptian and Assyrian sculpture, safe and secure eighty-six feet beneath the city streets.

During the previous week, similar scenes were acted out all across the Capital. At all the great national museums and galleries – the Science Museum, the National Portrait Gallery, the Royal Armouries, the Museum of London, the Imperial War Museum, the Maritime Museum, the Tate and Wallace collections, the Public Record Office and the Royal Palaces – wartime evacuation plans prepared as early as 1933 swung into action. By the time the German army rolled into Poland the museums and galleries of London were empty, echoing shells. In Trafalgar Square just empty, dusty frames adorned the walls of the National Gallery, while in Bloomsbury the few artefacts too large for rapid removal were bricked up where they stood in the British Museum.

The museums and galleries were not the only institutions enacting their emergency plans that autumn. A Reuters news report, circulated worldwide on 30 August 1939 described the scene in London:

Scores of banks and business houses are removing their headquarters and documents to the country, Lloyds are going to Salisbury, some Australian banks to Cobham in Surrey, and stockbrokers and others to Devonshire. The most valuable specimens from the Natural History Museum at Kensington have been transported to the country and the Tate Gallery has taken similar action. Furniture vans are removing furniture from the Foreign Office and other great buildings.

When contingency plans were first prepared it was thought that, when war came, only London and the south-east of England would be vulnerable to bombing. The museums and galleries evacuation plan, therefore, amounted to little more than the identification of suitable country houses, often the homes of museum Trustees or others in their social circle, considered far enough from London for safety, yet close enough for convenient transportation. Within a year though, following France's capitulation and the twin, equally unpalatable prospects of invasion or a long-drawn-out war, the original precautions were seen to be totally inadequate. Other factors, too, drove the Treasury and the Office of Works to seek safer subterranean storage; the remote, old country houses, as well as being now vulnerable to bombing, were seen as dangerous fire risks, and their owners – progressively more highly taxed as the war advanced – became increasingly fractious and uncooperative.

What began as a process of dispersal in the autumn of 1939 was abruptly reversed little more than a year later, and by 1942 the great cultural wealth of the nation was once again under the unified control of the Office of Works, concentrated in two vast, secret underground repositories in the high mountains of Wales and a remote river valley in rural Wiltshire. The detailed planning and implementation of this great evacuation of arts and treasures from the Capital, often in the face of profound opposition from the Treasury and the Service Ministries (who thought the money would be better spent on the direct prosecution of the war), is the central subject of the pages that follow.

2

INTER-WAR PLANS

During the early years of the twentieth century, despite the growing tensions between Britain and Germany – the consequence, in part at least, of the Teutonic urge to possess a seaborne military force that might challenge the supremacy of the British Navy – little thought was given to the possibility of an enemy invasion, and less still of the risk of aerial bombardment by enemy warplanes; a concept, indeed, hardly even imagined at that time. The Great War saw a sudden end to this complacency. During the first year of conflict German Zeppelin airships, though hydrogen-filled and vulnerable, ranged over Belgium, dropped primitive bombs fabricated from converted artillery shells and inflicted significant damage. A little later in the war the Zeppelins pottered more or less at will over London and eastern England, bombing haphazardly. Later still they were supplemented and then replaced by twin-engine Gothas and huge four-engined Staacken R.VI biplanes, the latter capable of carrying two tons of bombs and mounting true, strategic air-raids against Britain.

Although of minor consequence when compared with the intensive bombing of the early years of the Second World War, these raids caused some consternation in the government and resulted in several hastily convened committees to look into various air raid precautions to minimize the risks. Both the War Office and Ministry of Munitions realized from an early stage that underground storage offered the only absolute protection against aerial bombardment, but they also realized that the financial burden of providing such protection on a comprehensive scale was quite unviable. Limited underground protection was provided for the most vulnerable classes of explosives; both Ridge Quarry near Corsham in Wiltshire and Chislehurst caves were used to store part of the accumulating surplus of high explosives and propellants from Woolwich Arsenal and an underground magazine was excavated at the vast new filling factory built towards the end of the war at Chilwell near Nottingham.

Meanwhile the Office of Works, in consultation with several of the London museums, set up a special Air Raids Precaution Committee to look into the safe keeping of the nation's art treasures in the event of aerial attack. An operable plan was quickly developed and, under the joint management of the Office of Works and the Treasury, this was implemented quickly and efficiently. The most vulnerable books, documents and delicate ephemera from the British Museum were despatched into the custody of the National Library of Wales at Aberystwyth, while sturdier items were transferred to twenty-five basement strongrooms in Bloomsbury or packed in wooden crates to be stored in the West Central District station of the unfinished Post Office Underground Railway in Holborn. Other sections of the GPO tube system, completion of which had been temporarily suspended during the war, were also utilized; pictures from the Tate Gallery and the National Portrait Gallery, together with material from the Public Record Office, were stored in the station tunnels at King Edward's Building, while the Post Office station at Paddington held numerous pictures from the Royal Collection and porcelain from various royal residences. In a manner that was to be repeated in the Second World War, the National Gallery went its own way somewhat to the exasperation of the Office of Works. C.J. Holmes, chairman of the gallery trustees, negotiated separately with the London Underground Electric Railway Company to occupy part of the Aldwych branch tube tunnels where ultimately three hundred of the gallery's pictures were secreted. Another section of tube tunnel in South Kensington was used by the Victoria and Albert Museum to store a small part of its collection during the latter years of the war.

After the Armistice most of the artefacts were quickly returned to their respective museums and galleries and by 1920 the Army had cleared and abandoned its small number of wartime underground stores. A post-war committee to 'Consider the Revisions of the Regulations for Magazines and Care of War Materials' concluded in 1919 that the only safe storage for ammunition was deep underground but, as we have seen, this was an option that could not be afforded, so its findings were quietly filed and forgotten. Similarly, planning for the future safety of the nation's cultural heritage slipped back into quiescent lassitude for a decade or more. All this was to change at the end of January 1933 when Adolf Hitler became Chancellor of Germany and all the nations of Europe started to tread the long but inevitable road to war. Over the next two years the Army began actively planning the huge underground ammunition depots at Corsham – the biggest of their kind in the world – and the Admiralty put pressure on the Treasury for funding for its own multi-million pound underground magazines at Dean Hill near Salisbury and Trecwn in west Wales. Two years later the Air Ministry began construction of the first of its great underground reserve bomb dumps at Chilmark, to the west of Salisbury. On the civil front, too, preparations began and on 20 July 1933 the first meeting of the Museums and Galleries Air Raid Precautions Committee sat under the chairmanship of Lord Harlech, the First Commissioner of H.M. Office of Works.

In earlier informal discussions it had been decided that, in view of the fact that current military analysis indicated that German aircraft would be unable to penetrate further than London and the south-east counties, the best way to assure the safety of London's art treasures would be a policy of dispersal to the countryside. The first task of the ARP committee was, therefore, to ensure that

A list of recommended Country Houses etc where treasures could be stored would be prepared by the Office of Works and circulated to the Museums, etc. Directors would be invited to add to or comment on the list. The ultimate choice would be determined having regard, inter alia, to the non-proximity of military objectives likely to be the targets for bombs.

The selected places should be large and substantially built Country Seats in areas comparatively safe from aerial attack. Such houses should be remote from railways, large towns, aerodromes or military establishments, reasonably free from the risk of fire, and should be continuously maintained by a permanent staff of servants. The houses should also be capable of providing one or two large dry rooms with floors of sufficient strength to carry a number of cases of exhibits.

A list of some fifty country houses (the 'National Register') that might be suitable to house evacuated art treasures was drawn up and discreet enquiries made to their owners to gauge their acquiescence. The responses were generally encouraging, although somewhat lacklustre, the lack of enthusiasm due, perhaps, to a general feeling that to be seen to be preparing for war might somehow provoke war. The reply from W. Ormsby Gore, whose awareness of current events through his association with the Office of Works was a little more enlightened, is typical. He wrote:

I would be more than pleased to allow 'valuable documents, sculpture etc' from the British Museum to find a resting place here in time of war, but trust the necessity may never arise again in our lives.

After the first flurry of activity the committee did not meet again until mid-January of the following year. Members present at the second sitting included:

- H. Isherwood Kay and Mr E. Glasgow of the National Gallery
- H.M. Hake of the National Portrait Gallery
- Colonel E.B. Mackintosh representing the Science Museum
- Sir Eric Maclagan of the Victoria and Albert Museum
- J.B. Manson of the Tate Gallery
- Mr Ffoulkes of the Tower Armouries
- Mr A. Esdaile, representing Sir John Forsdyke of the British Museum

The committee considered that in the next war London would be subject, from the very first day, to intensive air bombardment and that the Whitehall area would be the primary target with damage overspilling into Victoria and the surrounding districts. Thus the National Gallery in Trafalgar Square and the National Portrait Gallery would be most at risk, the Tate much less so.

Initial plans to remove all the pictures and artefacts from every

London collection to Hampton Court Palace was quickly abandoned as the obvious folly of putting all ones eggs in the same basket was realized. Thereafter, more rational evacuation and dispersal schemes were discussed. It was suggested that the British Museum should be allocated a special train to take their most valuable books, manuscripts and other more delicate material to Aberystwyth, where the museum had already been preparing evacuation arrangements with the National Library of Wales. A proposal to use lorries was put forward as an alternative to rail transport but it was thought that the allocated vehicles might be seized by panicking refugees fleeing the bombed city.

Sir Eric Maclagan of the V&A reminded the committee that his museum had occupied a disused tube branch line in South Kensington during the First World War and proposed that that could be again utilized, probably for the storage of ceramics. Major Eggar, of the Ministry of Works, however, commented that these tunnels might be required in war for 'essential personnel'.

Mr Ffoulkes of the Tower Armouries suggested that occupation of the mostly disused Aldwych Branch might be obtained for use as a repository of first resort, and subsequently used as a clearing-house.

The subject of the safety of the Crown Jewels and the treasures in Buckingham Palace was raised; this matter was referred to the Lord Chamberlain whose responsibility it was.

The committee next examined the list of country houses the owners of which had responded favourably to the enquiries made the previous year. To produce a basis for further planning, an arbitrary allocation of these properties was then made, even before the various houses were visited to assess their suitability.

PRELIMINARY LIST OF COUNTRY HOUSE ALLOCATIONS:

BRITISH MUSEUM

- Boughton House, Northants.
- Deene Park, Peterborough
- Drayton House, Northants
- Apethorpe Hall, Northants

NATIONAL GALLERY and NATIONAL PORTRAIT GALLERY

- Cliveden, Bucks
- Greenlands, Bucks
- Mentmore, Bucks
- Waddesdon Manor, Bucks
- Bowood House, Wiltshire
- Buscot Park, Berks
- Buckland House
- Lockinge House, Berks

TATE GALLERY

- Corsham Court, Wiltshire
- Hartham Park, Wiltshire

VICTORIA & ALBERT MUSEUM

- Somerley Park, Hampshire
- Longford Castle, Wiltshire

WALLACE COLLECTION

- Hall Barn, Bucks
- Dropmore House, Bucks

SCIENCE MUSEUM

- Basing Park, Hants
- Herriard Park, Hants

PUBLIC RECORD OFFICE

- Southill Park, Bedfordshire
- Icklewell Bury, Bedfordshire

MUSEUM OF LONDON

- Ascott House, Bucks

IMPERIAL WAR MUSEUM

- Penn House
- Melchett Court

TOWER OF LONDON

- Ffoulkes considered it unnecessary to move exhibits from the Tower so no initial allocation was made.

It was questioned whether locations more remote from London would be required, but the general opinion was that this would not be necessary, although, as we have seen, the British Museum had already made contingency plans for the National Library of Wales at Aberystwyth, and the Victoria & Albert Museum had its own fleet of vans for extended journeys should they become necessary.

While the Museums and Galleries ARP Committee was developing joint evacuation plans for the London museums as a whole, the National Gallery was making alternative, independent arrangements for the safeguarding of its pictures. On 16 June 1933 the Trustees of the National Gallery wrote to the Treasury:

At a Board meeting of the Gallery it was resolved that a definite plan should be formed immediately for the safeguarding of the pictures of the National Gallery in the threat of war, and I am instructed to communicate with the Lords Commissioners of His Majesty's Treasury seeking their advice and cooperation in framing this plan.

This request prompted a rash of correspondence between the Treasury and the Cabinet Office, who previously had been unaware of the museum and gallery plans, seeking to establish upon whom the financial burden of the ARP preparations would ultimately fall. An investigation by the Cabinet Office revealed that the government, through the agency of the Board of Education, was directly responsible for:

• Victoria & Albert Museum
• Science Museum
• Bethnal Green Museum

Those establishments in receipt of grant-aid but responsible to a Board of Trustees included:

• British Museum
• British Museum Natural History Department
• Imperial War Museum
• Museum of London
• National Gallery
• National Portrait Gallery
• Wallace Collection

The constitution of the Admiralty Museum at Greenwich was found to be so convoluted that financial responsibility was never properly resolved. Worried that it might be committed to expenditure that had not been properly authorized, the Treasury requested from the Cabinet Office some clarification of the National Gallery scheme and the larger, more general Museums and Galleries ARP plans. In reply, Wing Commander Hodsell of the Cabinet Office informed the Treasury on 27 June that the Gallery had gone ahead unilaterally with its evacuation plan and that:

The Office of Works representative, Mr Eggar, reports that, as a matter of fact, he has been in touch with the National Gallery and has gone as far as to select personally those pictures which ought to be moved to safer places. Owing, however, to changes in personnel, it rather looks as if the tentative arrangements made had been mislaid.

Towards the end of 1934 licensing agreements had been made between the Office of Works, who were to look after the interests of the museums and galleries, and the London Passenger Transport Board for the use of certain disused tube tunnels, including the Aldwych branch, (which was earmarked for the British Museum), Down Street and Brompton Road, which was reserved for the Victoria & Albert Museum. It was recognized, however, that these tube tunnel repositories were only suitable for a limited range of artefacts and that the majority would have to be evacuated to the country.

Little more was heard of the ARP plans for nearly two years and the museums and gallery committee did not sit again until December 1936. Sir Eric Maclagan, for the British Museum, commented that it was quite possible that the next war might begin with a surprise attack, leaving little time to implement a major evacuation. He suggested that, while the use of tube tunnels such as those at Aldwych should be further investigated, there were severe limitations to their usefulness, and that a second line of defence – the provision of 'armoured refuges' within the museums themselves – should be considered. During the First World War twenty-five rooms in the cellars at Bloomsbury had been strengthened to safeguard British Museum exhibits against Zeppelin attacks and similar measures could be taken in anticipation of the next war. MacLagan's primary criticism of the Aldwych tube concerned access, which would only be available via the existing public lift shafts, and these were in commercial use until 11.30 pm each night. The LPTB stressed that these lifts were, anyway, only suitable for medium weight loads, and that heavy items would have to be delivered by road to their Lillie Bridge depot for despatch via night-time ballast train. A further problem with Aldwych was that the platforms and running tunnels were fifty-five feet below Thames high water making them highly susceptible to inundation.

A scheme to provide strengthened basements beneath most of the London galleries was prepared and put to the Treasury for approval. Sir Patrick Duff, Lord Harlech's successor at the Office of Works, explained to the Treasury that while evacuation to country houses remained the principal means of safeguarding the nation's treasures,

> It is recognized, however, that the evacuation scheme cannot be regarded as a complete solution of the problem, even so far as portable exhibits only are concerned, since many of these are of such a nature that a lengthy journey into the country could only be undertaken at a serious risk of damage and the possibility must also be visualized of an air attack occurring before the evacuation of exhibits selected for removal could be completed. A scheme 'B' has therefore been prepared for providing in each building strengthened storage space which, although not proof against a direct hit by a heavy high explosive bomb, would effect reasonable security against splinters, gas, fire, flood and the effects of blast. This could be used in the first place for the temporary concentration of exhibits awaiting removal, and subsequently for the fragile exhibits to be retained.

The estimated costs of these strengthening works were:

- British Museum £255
- National Gallery £1000
- National Portrait Gallery £380
- Victoria & Albert £515
- Wallace Collection £725
- Imperial War Museum £280

Fears were aroused that keeping the artefacts within the city might expose them to poison gas, and the chemical effects of gas upon the paintings in particular was a matter of considerable concern. A special National Gallery committee was formed to look into this problem, but its findings were never circulated.

Up until this time none of the Air Raid Precaution schemes had progressed beyond the planning stage and it was not until international tension heightened in the summer of 1938 that the first concrete measures were undertaken. Towards the end of May a Treasury grant of £1,140, somewhat above the earlier estimate, was made to the Wallace Collection for the strengthening of the ground floor and basement of Hertford House in Manchester Square, the property which, along with its collection of antiquities, was bequeathed to the nation by the widow of the late Sir Richard Wallace in 1897. The main work involved replacing the wood flooring on the ground floor with a concrete slab and alterations to the drainage system to obviate the risk of flooding.

During the following month the cellar strongrooms were reinstated at the British Museum, a special bomb-proof room was prepared in the basement of the Victoria and Albert Museum, and £1,370 was spent on preparing bomb-proof accommodation within the National Gallery. Provision here amounted to the replacement of existing wooden doors with steel doors near the intersection of two ground-floor passageways to form an armoured corridor. Describing the new works to the Board of Trustees, Sir Kenneth Clark explained that:-

The proposed strengthened storage space is to be formed out of two corridors which cross on the ground floor. Until an emergency arises these corridors and the rooms adjoining will be in use, and the steel doors will be hooked back; the wooden doors being used in their place. In time of emergency the steel doors (of the type designed for air-raid shelters) will be brought into operation and provide the necessary protection against blast, splinters, gas, fire and flood.

The first test of these arrangements occurred in October 1938 at the time of the Munich Crisis when two railway containers full of National Gallery pictures – approximately three hundred in all – were despatched to the National Library of Wales at Aberystwyth and the Prichard Jones Hall of the University of Wales at Bangor. The evacuation was accomplished without a hitch, a result perhaps of the two practice runs completed a few weeks earlier and a larger-scale experiment conducted the previous autumn. All the pictures were returned to London by 20 October. A handwritten note by Sir Kenneth Clark, attached to a railway invoice forwarded to the Treasury

> £59 3s 6d for taking certain pictures from the National Gallery to North Wales during the emergency and bringing them back afterwards,

reads:

> I enclose two railway accounts; that from the Great Western Railway seems reasonable, that from the LMS remarkably generous. All the special services which they gave us for the protection of the pictures have been given free and they have simply charged us as if the pictures were sacks of coal.

Although procedures for the country house evacuations for institutions other than the National Gallery remained untested, (indeed most of the earmarked houses had still not been visited by museum staff at the end of 1938), the Munich Crisis did highlight some of the deficiencies of the existing plans and gave a new impetus to the various tube tunnel schemes. One of the problems encountered at the National Gallery was that of quickly removing paintings from the gallery walls and manoeuvring the pictures in their heavy frames out of the building and into transport containers. Sir Kenneth Clark put forward a plan to adapt the majority of the gallery's picture frames so that the canvases could be quickly removed on lightweight 'flats', leaving the heavy ornate frames attached to the wall for later removal. The difficulty was that this would cost money that the Treasury would not readily sanction. However, Clark wrote to the Treasury asking:

> Due to an interregnum in the posts of Keeper of the National Gallery and Director of the Tate, there is cash to spare in the budget. Can this be used to adapt the picture frames?

The Treasury agreed to this arrangement and by September 1939 virtually all the pictures were in quick-release frames.

PROBLEMS DOWN THE TUBES

On 13 June 1938 members of the ARP committee, amongst them Sir John Forsdyke of the British Museum, accompanied by Dr Plenderleith, his Chief Scientific Officer, three representatives from the Public Record Office and four officers from the Office of Works, inspected the Aldwych tube tunnel. The PRO was to have joint custody of the tunnel for the duration of the war with the British Museum, while the Office of Works would be responsible for overseeing any alterations required to render the area suitable for storage, and would ultimately foot the bill.

Accommodation consisted of 1,800 feet of tunnel approximately eleven feet in diameter, divided into two sections of unequal length, with a live line crossing at the junction. The longest section was 1,500 feet. The general impression was that the location was not entirely suitable, being damp, with a high humidity and copious seepage water which would make it necessary to contain anything stored there in special sealed boxes. The British Museum representatives thought that packing items into watertight boxes would be too time-consuming in an emergency, but nevertheless went ahead with the purchase of 1,000 such boxes, each 20″ x 20″ x 40″ from the 'No-Nails' Box Company of Liverpool at a discounted price of 5s (25p) each. Access had earlier been identified as a potential difficulty due to the limited capacity of the lifts, and further investigation proved that even via the station lifts the Holborn end of the tunnel was almost inaccessible except via a long route from Aldwych station.

The Victoria & Albert Museum's problems at Brompton Road were much worse. As early as 1934 the Office of Works had arranged a licence agreement with the LPTB for the Victoria & Albert Museum to occupy parts of the disused Brompton Road tube station as an emergency repository in time of war. However, when, following the Munich Crisis in October 1938, the time came to act upon this agreement, a V&A inspection team were disconcerted when they arrived on site to discover the Army already in residence. The underground station consisted of two running tunnels with separate platforms accessed by two parallel passageways leading, respectively, from the front and rear of three vertical lift shafts. The licence granted to the Victoria & Albert Museum allowed sole occupation of one of these access tunnels for storage. Questioned by Sir John Forsdyke, the Commanding Officer of No. 1 AA Company, whose unit was found in occupation of the greater part of the station complex, explained that the War Office had in fact purchased the freehold of the underground station, the three lift shafts and the surface building for £24,000 as it was 'ideally situated and a most suitable site for the Gun Operations Room of the Inner London Anti-Aircraft Zone'. He then went on to explain that:

> He proposed to use just one tunnel, leaving the other free for art treasures, and that he had no intention of storing ammunition or explosives underground, it was just to be an operations room for the Inner London AA zone.

Further investigation made on 23 November indicated, however, that the army had installed 'cables and certain signals contrivances' that completely blocked the entrance to the tunnel the V&A intended to use. The Office of Works launched an inquiry into the events at Brompton Road and subsequently Sir Patrick Duff wrote to Sir Herbert Creedy at the War Office:

My people have paid a visit to the tunnel with Colonel Wickens and they find that it is proposed to use the tunnel, of which we hold a license, for telephone apparatus etc, and the other tunnel for ventilation purposes, so that although the station has been sold to the War Department subject to our license, this has in practice been brushed aside.

Accepting that the fault did not lie entirely with the War Department, Duff continued:

The fact remains, however, that we are left holding the baby; a vital part of the co-ordinated arrangements for protecting the nation's art treasures, on which we had been hard at work for two or three years has broken down, and the accommodation earmarked on our register has been taken away from us just when it was needed. In view of the large sum of money which you are spending on your scheme we must, I suppose, agree to the cancellation of our licence and start all over again. It is very disappointing.

Subsequently the Commanding Officer wrote to Sir John Forsdyke:

I am sorry that Anti-Aircraft work was allowed to go ahead at the station without the people concerned or yourselves fully understanding each others requirements, but this work is in fact of very vital importance in our defence scheme and it is this, and not the question of the money spent on it, that makes it imperative that we continue.

AN UNWELCOME INTERVENTION BY THE NATIONAL LIBRARY OF WALES

A prominent, Treasury-inspired characteristic of the inter-war plans for safeguarding the nation's art treasures was that, whatever else, they had to be capable of implementation as cheaply as possible. The art treasures problem was perceived as being very much in second place to the material prosecution of war and there was a distinct impression that worrying about elitist, artistic trifles when the safety of the State was in question was somehow unpatriotic. Both the Cabinet Office and the Treasury wanted at all costs to avoid the necessity of providing purpose-built underground shelters for museum and art gallery artefacts. By the end of 1938 the Treasury and War Office were involved in bitter recrimination over the cost of the underground ammunition depots at Corsham that had already exceeded their estimated costs by a factor of ten, with the majority of the work still unfinished. Underground building projects were anathema to the Treasury, and officers there were appalled by the contents of a letter received on 28 May 1938 from W. Llewellyn Davies, Librarian of the National Library of Wales, requesting funding for just such a project at Aberystwyth. A new library building had been completed the previous year; one third of the construction cost was provided by a bequest from the late Sir John Williams and the rest in the form of a Treasury grant. Llewellyn Davies considered that the cost of constructing an underground bomb shelter for the library might be paid as an extension of this grant, and wrote:

> I am directed by the Council of the National Library of Wales to make application to His Majesty's Treasury for a Grant-in-Aid towards the cost of an Air Raid Precautions chamber for the protection in the event of danger from air raids, of some of the more valuable literary and historical treasures which this Library holds in trust for the Welsh Nation. We have decided upon the construction of such a chamber in the form of a tunnel of suitable form and dimension excavated in the rock slopes of the hill upon which the Library is built and in close proximity to the building itself.

Llewellyn Davies estimated that the proposed tunnel, which would be approximately one hundred feet in length and fully air-conditioned, would cost £3,500 to build. He continued:

> In the event of an emergency arising the National Library of Wales would be prepared to house valuable manuscripts, etc, from some of the more important libraries in England. In fact, a request of this nature has already been received from one of the Cambridge libraries. It will be recalled that the National Library of Wales was able to take care of some of the most valuable collections of the British Museum during the last war.

Sir John Forsdyke chaired a small sub-committee of the Museum and Galleries ARP committee that was advising national and provincial museums on inexpensive means of strengthening cellars, etc, to protect their artefacts against enemy bombing. Mr H.B. Usher, the recipient of Llewellyn Davies' letter, immediately contacted Sir John in the hope that he might dissuade the National Library of Wales from pressing for underground accommodation and might follow a more economic route. On 16 June Usher wrote:

> We do not quite see how we could make a Grant without exposing ourselves to similar demands over a very wide field.
> It has occurred to me that it might be helpful if, when we reply to the National Library of Wales, we could say something about your little committee. Do you think we could tell them that there is such a committee sitting and that it may have suggestions to make which will be helpful to them in considering their local problem – or something to that effect?

Forsdyke's reaction to the letter was not at all what Usher expected. Rather than support the Treasury's parsimonious policy Sir John used the opportunity offered by Llewellyn Davies' letter roundly to criticize all the measures so far proposed, writing strongly that:

> *The letter from the National Library of Wales raises questions which go beyond that institution. No safe repositories have been constructed for the protection of any National Property* [works of art, literature or records] *against High Explosive or Incendiary bombs. The National Gallery has a newly finished shelter* [the 'armoured corridor'] *which it describes as 'Bomb-Proof', but the Office of Works tells me that it is not so. In fact the Office of Works has told us from the start that the provision of safe storage on the premises is impossible. They are giving us splinter-proof or shock-proof basements (costing in my own case £250), and various country houses for the storage of our most valuable material.*
>
> *A report by my Research Chemist upon the Aldwych-Holborn tube, which is allotted to the British Museum and the Public Records Office bears out what I have always understood, that this will not do for books and manuscripts. That is to say, the National Library and the Public Record Office have no provision made for them except the country houses, which may or may not be damp-proof, fire- and burglar-proof, and in my own case the National Library of Wales, which has formally granted us a certain amount of accommodation as it did in the First War.*
>
> *One really bomb-proof repository for perishable National Treasures of supreme importance ought to be provided somewhere, preferably as part of a national institution which already has the machinery for safe custody and warding.*

Further into his letter, he specifically criticizes the Aldwych tube tunnel, which, he says, will require the construction of bulkheads against gas and flooding which would make movement within the repository almost impossible, and further asserted that:

> *It would be futile to attempt to condition the air of the storage accommodation because it is not possible to ensure that the electricity supply would not be cut off in emergency, and the necessary plant could not be effectively run on an auxiliary supply.*

The Aberystwyth debate caused an immediate crisis at the Treasury and a rash of intemperate correspondence. Eric de Normann at the Office of Works was in a difficult position. It was his task to look after the interests and safety of the national museums and galleries, but also to minimize the demands his department made upon exchequer funds. He had been long aware of the dissatisfaction of Sir John Forsdyke and others regarding the proposed ARP measures and had communicated this to Gilbert, who was Usher's superior at the Treasury. On 22 June Usher replied to de Normann, with reference to Sir John Forsdyke's letter:

> *From your letter to Gilbert of 15th June, I gather that you have feared that some such proposal for further underground storage accommodation*

might be forthcoming.

Within the Treasury there was a profound feeling that the request from the National Library of Wales could not be met. Usher minuted that it would be politically dangerous to meet the library's demands and that:

It might also open the door to applications from provincial institutions and even perhaps the Universities.

We could scarcely give the National Library of Wales – a grant-aided body in a pre-eminently safe position – the perfectly bomb-proof shelter which we have denied to the great National Museums and Galleries.

Eric de Normann reiterated Usher's views, commenting in a memo to the Treasury:

To come to the request of the National Library of Wales at Aberystwyth; what I am afraid of is that once you have admitted the principle of giving so-called bomb-proof underground accommodation to a comparatively unimportant institution, you will have trouble in resisting similar demands from the great Museums and Galleries. They are, as you know, immense collections, and to provide underground accommodation would cost a most formidable total.

Are there no existing cellars or basements in the National Museum of Wales that could be strengthened to serve the purpose? Aberystwyth, I imagine, must be one of the safest places in the country, as there can be no economic targets there.

To sum up; if you think you must give the British Museum underground accommodation for historic treasures, this proposal sounds cheap, if the figure is right. There is, I expect, a good deal of underground accommodation in England generally, if one could only get to know about it, but one would always have to face the difficulty of damp.

Gilbert, too, was of the opinion that to comply with the National Library of Wales' request would set an unacceptable precedent. Writing on 28 July he stated bluntly:

I have no doubt that this should be rejected completely, for the following reasons:

(a) The cost of ARP for the general public will in the main depend upon 'shelter policy'; at present this is to provide blast-proof and splinter-proof accommodation. If we are driven to a higher scale of protection the cost will be enormous, and the provision of an underground bomb-proof shelter in Aberystwyth for art treasures would hardly strengthen our hand in resisting similar shelters; e.g – in London for human beings.

(b) In all ARP we have gone on the basis of assuming some period of warning – and I should have thought that arrangements for the safe

accommodation of Art Treasures should only be planned now, so as to enable them to be put into rapid execution in any war. Minor structural precautions and the provision of sandbags should be the most that was executed in peacetime.

Forsdyke's campaign for more secure underground accommodation, despite increasing support from outsiders including the Archbishop of Canterbury, had little effect upon the Treasury. Eventually, however, it was agreed that if the tunnel proposed by the National Library of Wales was designated as a general storage facility for all the national museums and galleries rather than just for the NLW, then a small grant towards its construction might be justified. Within the Treasury, though, it was feared that:

The National Library of Wales is probably thinking in terms of books, and a tunnel big enough for them might be very small for National Treasures.

With the aid of a £3,500 grant, excavations began earlier the following year for what was intended to be a tunnel one hundred feet long and eight feet high in a slate escarpment within the Library grounds. Shortly after work began it was discovered that the rock strata was very badly broken and within a short while all the available money was used up on remedial works and no more was forthcoming. The finished tunnel, which was the only underground protection for art treasures completed before the outbreak of war, was a very poor thing – at fifty-six feet in length only half its intended capacity and with only the most rudimentary services installed.

The general view of the government was that Sir John Forsdyke was something of a thorn in its side who put the varying requirements of the museums and galleries above the greater national interest. It was thought that Forsdyke had failed to produce a unified, inexpensive plan for safeguarding the treasures within the Capital and had instead allowed each gallery to implement its own independent scheme. Such a standardized approach as the Treasury had in mind would, of course, have been quite unworkable given the broad range of artefacts drawn under the protection of the Museums and Galleries Air Raid Precautions Committee, which included paintings and drawings ranging from the fragile Leonardo cartoons to the huge Veroneses and Van Dycks in the National Gallery, and from delicate textiles to the monolithic Assyrian sculptures in the British Museum that were so large that the only option was to brick them up where they stood for the duration of the war. The rather haphazard measures that most of the museums, with the exception of the National Gallery, took to protect their contents at the time of the Munich Crisis reinforced the government's current critical opinion. John Beresford, chairman of the ARP Standing Committee on Museums and Galleries, writing in a preface to the standing committee's report to the Treasury in January 1939, considered that:

It is perhaps typical of the peculiar way in which the National Museums and Galleries conduct their affairs that Forsdyke's committee as such apparently dedicated its energies mainly to the provincial problem [i.e the question raised by the National Museum of Wales]. *Meanwhile each of the National institutions proceeded separately with their own arrangements during the Munich Crisis.*

In the hopelessly un-coordinated world of the National Museums and Galleries my principle has been to cling like grim death to the one departmental rock (for this particular purpose) in a weary land, namely the Office of Works.

What in our judgement is imperatively necessary is to knock the heads of the Directors together, and endeavour to force them to collaborate one and all with the Office of Works. All I want from the Treasury is an informal blessing to what we have attempted to do. Any Treasury objections at this stage would frankly tempt me to throw up an almost unspeakable sponge!

Beresford's report stressed the utmost importance of the Office of Works being regarded as the central co-ordinating authority for all accommodation and transport requirements of the National Museums and Galleries. It also advised that rail transport should be used for emergency evacuation of art treasures as:

many of us think that road transport would be unsafe in the stress of general evacuation of urban areas, unless lorries had military guards or were otherwise marked as inviolable Government vehicles.

In sharp contrast to what was considered an otherwise disorganized fiasco, the National Gallery's evacuation to North Wales during the Munich period was held as an excellent example of transport practice.

Despite all the difficulties, tangible progress had been made with the ARP preparations by the early spring of 1939. The Victoria & Albert had lost Brompton Road but had been granted the finance for a 2,000 square-foot 'bomb-proof chamber', construction of which was completed by 2 February, in the basement of its Kensington premises. The National Gallery had already rehearsed its plans to occupy parts of the National Library of Wales and the Pritchard Jones Hall of the University of Wales. The British Museum had completed the strengthening of its Bloomsbury basement and had come to an agreement with the London Passenger Transport Board to occupy the Aldwych tube tunnel. The museum had also reached agreement with the Welsh National Library to jointly occupy the less-than-satisfactory tunnel at Aberystwyth. Meanwhile, the Science Museum had begun work on its own strengthened basement, which was completed in August 1939.

The National Maritime Museum intended to maintain most of its collection in London, protected within a sandbagged basement and semi-basement shelter which was sanctioned by the Treasury early in September 1939. However, following severe bomb damage to the Museum on the night of 8/9 December 1940, this was rendered unusable and:

> *The Trustees have consequently decided that it will be best to remove at least a selection of the pictures to Dunster Lodge in Somerset, where some of the exhibits for which they are responsible have already been stored. The house is the property of Messrs Spink, of 6 King Street, St James, who have their most reliable and most trusted employees there to maintain constant watch and ward over their property.*

Plans were drawn up as early as January 1937 for the establishment of a bomb-proof shelter for the Tate Gallery in the basement of the new Duveen Gallery which was nearing completion at that time. This was initially considered an ideal location as the floor above, which was a four-inch-thick reinforced concrete slab, was massively supported by eighteen-inch-square steel and concrete piles. It was then realized that the basement was some ten feet below Thames flood level, and that if the river retaining wall was breached by a bomb the cellars would be immediately inundated. The feasibility of strengthening the river defences with flood-boards was examined briefly but rejected on account of its aesthetic impact. Tests soon indicated, anyway, that if watercolours were stored in the basement strong room for more than twenty-four hours the high humidity would do irreversible damage. Subsequently it was arranged that pictures from the Tate would go immediately to country house repositories in Herefordshire and Northumberland, whilst some of the sculpture and other items would find refuge in a disused subway at the Piccadilly tube station.

The question of the security of treasures from Buckingham Palace and Windsor Castle, essentially a private collection owned by the Royal Family, was raised by Sir Hill Child in September 1938. Earlier he had discussed the matter of the paintings from the Royal Collection with Sir Kenneth Clark who advised that as an immediate measure steps should be taken to ensure the safety of at least fifty-nine of the best pictures. Hill Child wrote to Eric de Normann at the Office of Works requesting guidance regarding a safe refuge for the pictures, and also contacted Sir Patrick Duff, the First Commissioner, to whom he wrote:

> *My dear Duff, can you suggest any building in charge of the Office of Works where some valuable china and other objects of art could be stored in comparative safety in the event of war – I feel that any severe bombing near the Palace would probably break or crack china?*
>
> *I am not in favour of sending china from here to Windsor. The castle is already full of china and other valuables and I think it a mistake to put*

all our eggs in one basket. I don't imagine the Royal Residences would be specially selected for bombing, but, if they were, Windsor Castle on the bank of the river would be a very tempting target.

Sir Patrick had earlier made it well known that in his opinion the safety of the Royal Collection and the Crown Jewels to be the responsibility of the Lord Chamberlain and not the Office of Works, but after some delay he offered space in the Dover Street tube tunnel to the Palace, but warned Sir Hill Child, with a hint of mild sarcasm:

Dear Child, the Dover Street tunnel is primarily intended for the Museum of London though I understand space is to be provided for china from Buckingham Palace. There would of course be some vibration from passing trains.

3

THE COUNTRY HOUSES

Although the National Register of potentially eligible country houses had been compiled many years earlier it was not until the early months of 1939 that any detailed inspections were made. The final allocations, detailed below, were agreed on 1 September and were fairly closely adhered to:

IMPERIAL WAR MUSEUM

PENN HOUSE, Amersham
COLWORTH HOUSE, Sharnbrook
RAMSTER, Chiddingfold, Surrey

NATIONAL GALLERY

PRITCHARD JONES HALL (University of Wales, Bangor)
NANTEOS, Aberystwyth
OLD QUARRIES, Avening, Gloucestershire
CROSSWOOD HOUSE, Aberystwyth
NANT CLWYD HALL, Ruthin
PENRYHN CASTLE, Caernarvonshire
COED COCH, Abergele, Conway
BODRHYDDAN, Rhyl
BODFEAN, Pwllheli
NATIONAL LIBRARY OF WALES, Aberystwyth (Distribution Centre)

WALLACE COLLECTION

HALL BARN, Buckinghamshire
BALLS PARK, Hertfordshire

LONDON MUSEUM

ASCOTT HOUSE, Buckinghamshire

BRITISH MUSEUM

BOUGHTON HOUSE, Northamptonshire
DRAYTON HOUSE, Northamptonshire

The British Museum had initially been allocated three additional houses from the *National Register*, but on 28 March 1939 Sir John Forsdyke informed the Office of Works that:

I have now decided that of the five Country Houses which were assigned to us by the First Commissioner in 1934 as war repositories, Boughton House and Drayton House [both near Kettering] *will be enough for our purposes.*

VICTORIA & ALBERT MUSEUM

MONTACUTE HOUSE, Somerset

TATE GALLERY

MUNCASTER CASTLE, Cumberland
HELLENS, Much Marcle, Herefordshire
EASTINGTON HALL, Worcestershire

Hartham Park and Corsham Court in Wiltshire had first been proposed as repositories for the Tate Gallery, but the proximity of the Central Ammunition Depot and other military installations in the vicinity of Corsham made the area inherently unsafe.

NATIONAL PORTRAIT GALLERY

MENTMORE HOUSE, Buckinghamshire
BOWOOD HOUSE, Wiltshire

GEOLOGICAL MUSEUM

WALCOT HALL, Shropshire

SCIENCE MUSEUM

HERRIAND PARK, Basingstoke
RUTHERFORD PARK, Alton, Hampshire

NATURAL HISTORY MUSEUM

TRING PARK, Hertfordshire

INDIA OFFICE

ASKE, Richmond, Yorkshire

PUBLIC RECORD OFFICE

MARKET HARBOROUGH CASUALTY WARDS, Leicestershire
SHEPTON MALLET PRISON, Somerset
BELVOIR CASTLE, Leicestershire

FITZWILLIAM MUSEUM

GREDINGTON, Flintshire

'BRATS FROM BRISTOL'

It had been felt for some time by the museum trustees who were responsible for organizing their various ARP arrangements that the owners of certain country houses were working to their own private agendas in offering their homes as wartime repositories. Lord Ilchester, who was vice-chairman of the Museum Advisory Council on Air Raid Precautions was in particular suspected of such subterfuge. Shortly after it was agreed that Montacute House, a National Trust property in poor condition and virtually unoccupied, should be used by the Victoria & Albert Museum, it became known that the Home Office had earlier rejected the house as unsuitable, due to its poor condition, as a home for evacuee children. Lord Ilchester made great play of this fact, commenting to the ARP Advisory Council that:

> *Empty houses were the very place for evacuated children, but if Montacute is not safe for them it is certainly not safe for the V&A treasures.*

Ilchester launched a vociferous campaign against Montacute, claiming that, among other things, its proximity to the recently established Westland aircraft factory at Yeovil, some six miles distant, made the house vulnerable to enemy bombing. This greatly annoyed Sir Eric Maclagan, Director of the V&A, who responded testily:

> *I have always felt that whatever place we selected as a refuge would almost inevitably have a training camp or an aircraft factory built at once in its neighbourhood.*

Ilchester continued his campaign to discredit Montacute and turned his tirade upon the Board of Education which was the government department that finally adjudicated upon such matters. In response to an inquiry from the Board, Maclagan replied on 20 February 1939 that:

> *Ilchester has been generating concern over the Westland factory and thus proposes his own home, Melbury House instead. We are inclined to think that his zeal is not wholly disinterested and that he hopes by sheltering the nation's treasures at Melbury to avoid having Brats from Bristol quartered on him. But this may be an unjust suspicion!*

The Duke of Buccleuch, owner of Boughton House near Kettering, the British Museum's most important country house repository, was discreetly advised by Sir John Forsdyke not to inquire too deeply into the advantages regarding immunity from evacuee children when discussing the use of his house for art treasures with the Office of Works. In the months leading up to the outbreak of war it was considered within the government to be unpatriotic, rather unseemly and not a little undemocratic to appear unwilling to share the coming burden equitably. In a letter to Mr Bennitt at the Office of Works, written in July 1939, Sir John Forsdyke said of the Duke of Buccleuch:

I also told him not to say anything to you about his billeting burdens, and I do not know if we can help him in this matter, or if we ought to help him. Not even a Duke can expect to get through the war without some suffering, and he recognizes that he suffers at Boughton a good deal less from us than he would do from anybody else; soldiers, or Gibraltar refugees or even a girl's school.

As general information about the Museums and Galleries evacuation plans leaked out, the various government departments involved in the project were inundated with offers from the owners of often quite unsuitable country houses that had not been included in the National Register in 1934. The naïve transparency of some of those offers – desperate attempts to avoid the perceived horrors of 'Brats from Bristol' or flea-ridden evacuee children from the east end of London – was often received with disdain. Typical of these was an offer from Mr G. Workman MacNaghten of the Manor House, Chew Magna in Somerset, addressed to the Secretary of the Treasury in February 1939:

I wish to offer this house as a repository for works of art and other articles from Museums in London which it may be desired to house in the country in the event of war. It is not, I think, a very suitable house for billeting children or evacuated adults as it has a large amount of Elizabethan and Jacobean oak carving and panelling, including a rather fine carved oak Jacobean staircase, carved stone and oak chimney pieces and so forth, apart from a library of 2,000 books, a great deal of armour and period furniture throughout the house.

The Treasury chose to make no immediate reply, so one week later MacNaghten renewed his assault, writing:

I have been given to understand that our water supply does not comply with the requirements of the Ministry of Health. We depend for our drinking water on a pump in the kitchen, which is the same system as has been used for 400 years, and while this would be considered good enough for two or three children in a cottage, it is not considered that it would be suitable for any considerable number of children billeted in a large house.

The Treasury made no further reply. Within a year, however, as previously unforeseen problems developed at the existing country house repositories and new locations were required to house the contents of provincial museums, the government's previously prim attitude relaxed markedly. By the late summer of 1940, with the prospect of imminent invasion, the Office of Works was openly touting to prospective landlords the advantages of using their properties as repositories for art. When the *National Register* was compiled in 1934 many in the Office of Works considered Earl Spencer's home at Althorp an ideal location; it already contained a substantial collection of antiquities and thus was, presumably, already provided with adequate security and fire-fighting facilities and had a resident staff experienced in the handling of *objets d'art*. But Earl Spencer had not offered his house to the museums and in August 1940 Sir Patrick Duff sought to cajole him into doing so, writing, with reference to houses already under museum occupation:

My dear Spencer... since they are being used for a National purpose, we have been able to keep them free from, say, evacuated children, and have discouraged their use for any purpose that might make them a military target or interfere with the works of art themselves. Beyond this all that we have done is see that fire precautions are adequate for safeguarding the national possessions, but the pictures etc have never been spread all over the houses and we have not regarded the houses as completely sterilized for other purposes.

Somewhat conciliatorily, Earl Spencer replied:

I did not offer this house as it is already so completely full of every kind of thing of my own. I could no doubt do so at a pinch, if I knew what sort of things they were.

Perhaps one of the most surprising aspects of the country house dispersal plan is that up until November 1939 there appears to have been absolutely no discussion of financial arrangements; it was expected by the Office of Works that the houses would be offered rent free by the owners and this was largely accepted. The fact that additional expenses above the normal running costs of a large house might be incurred in looking after the museum exhibits was either overlooked or ignored in the first instance and was to give rise to unfortunate disagreements as the war progressed. This situation seems to have arisen as a result of the prevalent, idealized vision of the aristocratic life style that was very much a rose-tinted hangover from the Edwardian era. Men in the Office of Works who knew no better imagined a typical country estate that was still a land of milk and honey ruled firmly but fairly by a paternalistic Lord, where cash still flowed aplenty, the great house maintained by armies of servants and gardeners and winter fires burned bright in every room. The reality, however, was much different, as the Office of Works was to report to the Treasury shortly after the first evacuations had got under way. Of the country houses, Sir Patrick Duff wrote:

As is not surprising, we have found that these places are not entirely suited as they stand to house very valuable 'treasures' which in addition are sometimes, as in the case of old pictures, highly perishable if exposed to conditions at all severe or exceptional.

The owners of Country Houses, owing to increased taxation as well as perhaps natural conservatism, have retained standards of lighting, heating and fire protection which are by no means always sufficient to preserve the exhibits from deterioration or to reduce the fire risk to a degree which can be accepted in respect of such priceless objects.

Other holes, too, began to appear in the untried dispersal plans which had been merely theoretical and dormant for the past five years. No thought had been given to the accommodation of museum staff who were expected to accompany and invigilate the artefacts; how, for instance, would such staff be integrated into existing evacuee schemes and would they be classified as evacuees themselves? Would they pay rent for their accommodation, would the landlords be paid a billeting allowance, or would board and lodging in the Big House be provided free of charge? At some locations, particularly those occupied by the British Museum, it was argued that museum staff resident there should be waited upon by the servants as if they were guests of the family. Elsewhere staff were denied even coal to heat their rooms unless they purchased it themselves. These were problems that were never properly resolved and gave rise to endless recriminations in the later years of the war.

Whilst they were quite happy to play host to the pictures and antiquities, many country house owners were unhappy about their homes being invaded by strangers and were fearful for the security of their own possessions given the influx of unknown personnel. There were fears too regarding the possibility of structural damage caused by the movement of large quantities of evacuated artefacts inside the houses. After visiting the two houses near Kettering occupied by the British Museum, an Office of Works representative noted that:

Access to one of our allocated rooms on the first floor at Boughton House is most conveniently gained through some of the State Apartments, and access to the whole of the upper floor of Drayton House is by way of a very beautiful oak spiral staircase which I am advised is itself of considerable antique and architectural value.

He went on to advise that 'a suitable cover should be provided for the staircase at Drayton House as protection against fire and malicious damage'.

Belated efforts were made by the Office of Works to formulate a general policy to deal with all financial claims that arose in respect of the country house repositories. An internal memo recommended that:

In concluding the financial arrangements, we should be authorized to include a reference to making good damages on the lines of a 'gentleman's agreement'. The Treasury Solicitor might perhaps be asked to advise on the exact terms of reference.

The Treasury, however, had little interest in framing any formula that might increase the final cost of the evacuation plans, a cost which it was determined to maintain at the lowest possible level. All such matters as compensation for incidental damage, claims for additional heating allowances, etc, were, as we shall see in the pages that follow, argued out individually and endlessly on a case by case basis by the local Office of Works representatives. By early 1941 at many of the country houses Treasury parsimony, increasing shortages of material and staff and the general pressures of war led to a level a brittle intolerance that in itself, almost as much as the increased threat of aerial bombardment, led to the eventual abandonment of the country house scheme and the adoption of what Sir John Forsdyke advocated from the first instance, the construction of purpose-built, universal underground bomb-proof shelters.

4

THE BRITISH MUSEUM

Sir John Forsdyke's pre-war campaign for purpose-built, bomb-proof underground storage for the nation's art treasures had largely fallen on deaf ears and had indeed evoked considerable criticism from some quarters. There was some tacit support for his scheme from Eric de Normann at the Office of Works who had made unofficial inquiries on Forsdyke's behalf into the possibility of securing storage space in a disused salt mine in Cheshire, owned by ICI. Forsdyke's enthusiasm for this scheme was tempered by doubts about the mine's location and means of access, which was via a 400-foot vertical shaft. In May he wrote to de Normann:

> As for your comment about the ICI salt mine. I am taking advice about the practical possibilities of this, but am inclined to think that there would be serious difficulties in the invigilation of valuable materials there. Also, we are well enough provided with repositories elsewhere if only we can get to them, and it will be no easier to get to Cheshire than to Northampton. The only advantage of the mine seems to be that it is really bomb-proof.

Sir John was hardly confident in his assertion that they were 'well enough provided with repositories', for later in the same letter he goes on to worry, 'are Boughton and Drayton too close to Corby for safety?' Two months later these fears were confirmed when, following a briefing at the Air Ministry, he told Sir Patrick Duff at the Office of Works:

> We are having to face the position that the two houses at Kettering [Drayton and Boughton] selected for the British Museum treasures are not sufficiently outside vulnerable areas, and we are advised to seek houses in Wales, away from the Swansea area, as has been done by the National Gallery. I can only note from our files two possibilities: Voelas at Betws-y-Coed, and St David's College at Lampeter.

Neither of these alternatives were suitable and during the ten days leading up to the outbreak of the Second World War the Treasures of the British Museum, save the few items that were relegated to the basement vaults, were distributed according to the 1934 schedule to the doubtful security of Drayton House, Boughton House, the National Library of Wales and the Aldwych tube.

Meanwhile, the question was raised regarding what measures should be taken to protect the larger exhibits in the museum, particularly the Assyrian frescoes and the six large winged Assyrian bulls which were too massive to transport. The former, it was decided, would be protected by a false wall of interlocking blocks, but the Assyrian bulls proved more contentious. The Treasury refused to sanction the cost of £2,125 required to brick them up, asking, 'Are they worth the expenditure and should they not be left to fend for themselves?'

On 18 August a further three thousand cases arrived at the Museum from the 'No-Nails' box company and the process of packing got under way. Fifty large railway containers arrived in the forecourt at Bloomsbury, twenty destined for Aberystwyth, the rest for Drayton and Boughton. Loading started in the early afternoon and the containers were filled approximately one per hour. The first were despatched to Aberystwyth that evening and, five days later, on 23 August, the first shipment made its way to Drayton House. Twenty larger type 'BK' containers destined for Boughton were filled at the rate of two per day, the last leaving on the evening of Friday, 1 September. The following night two specially prepared low-loader lorries carried the 100 tons of Elgin Marbles eight miles to Lillie Bridge yard, now packed securely in wooden crates, to await the evening ballast train to Aldwych.

Most of the museum's collection of books and manuscripts was sent to the National Library of Wales where they were stored in the new tunnel and in rooms on the upper floor of the building. A small part of the museum library, sealed in moisture-proof boxes, found temporary refuge alongside the Speaker's Plate from the House of Commons in Dover Street station, until packed off a few weeks later to join the crated Elgin Marbles in the Aldwych tube. At Boughton House the collection

The entrance to the small underground store built for the British Museum in the grounds of the National Library of Wales at Aberystwyth. In this view excavation of the tunnel has just begun.

An interior view of the Aberystwyth tunnel showing material from the British Museum library in store.

Sculpture from the British Museum being manhandled down a staircase at Aldwych tube station.

Boughton House near Kettering, home of the Duke of Buccleuch.

of coins and medals was heaped upon the floor of the kitchen, while other items – most of the remainder of the Bloomsbury artefacts – were stashed in an unfinished wing of the house which had walls and roof but no floors, poor ventilation and was unheated. Museum staff were unhappy about the concentration of so much of the nation's heritage in Boughton House, noting in a report to the Office of Works that:

> The weak point of Boughton is that it is putting all our best things together in a tinder box building where an odd oil-bomb would destroy the lot.

After the first few weeks of hectic activity, during which the expected

An interior view of the unfurnished wing at Boughton House, occupied by the British Museum during the early war years.

bombers had not come, museum staff at the country houses were able to take stock of their new surroundings. By November, with winter encroaching upon the countryside, it was apparent that the environmental conditions for the long-term storage of exhibits would have to be addressed. The Office of Works had not previously realized that under normal circumstances only small parts of the large country houses were adequately heated and they were faced with the interminable task of agreeing with the owners the allocation of additional heating and lighting costs. There was some concern that at present the property owners were footing the entire bill, but that such a situation was not sustainable. Eric de Normann put the case so:

> Regarding payment, the owners can be categorised thus: the National Library of Wales is a patient, corporate body; the Duke of Buccleuch is semi-corporate and less easy to deal with; Stopford-Sackville at Drayton House, for whom this is a purely personal matter, is very uneasy indeed.

The matter, however, was urgent for at Drayton House, where ethnographic items were stored in the unheated Chapel, the exhibits were growing mildew. The Stopford-Sackvilles lived in only one wing, which was partially heated, and the rest of the house was sealed off for most of the year. The ethnographic material at Drayton House required a temperature of 60° and, referring to both Boughton and Drayton, it was stated that:

> Both houses may require auxiliary heating for the protection of exhibits, I suggest low temperature tubular heating, officials in charge to decide if there is any possibility of the exhibits in their keeping deteriorating.

De Normann also noted that at Boughton they had 'already experienced £1,000 worth of loss for not spending £50.' The Office of Works had been quoted £50 for the installation of a heater that would raise the temperature to the required 55-60° but this had been refused by the Treasury.

At Drayton a lesser worry was the provision of adequate accommodation on site for the four staff members who were quartered in the disused wing of the house. Other problems emerged through the early winter months. There was some doubt whether the upper floors of the 300-year-old building were capable of taking the required weight of crated artefacts. A survey indicated that a large room over the King's Dining Room on the first floor was so rickety that it was unsafe for even light loads and the risk of woodworm was an ever-present threat. British Museum custodians there reported that 'specimens are treated daily with a liquid containing kerosene or similar' to allay the presence of the pest.

By January 1940 conditions had so deteriorated at Drayton House that the British Museum man there, F.J.E. Raby, had arranged for the ethnographic items to be removed from the Chapel into the Long Library on the upper floor of the inhabited section of the house. Six months later, with German bombers now ranging freely over the east midlands, the Long Library, with its ceiling open to the rafters, was judged too much of a fire risk. Sir John Forsdyke decided that, 'as there is no independent ceiling, so incendiary bombs could come through the slates and lodge in the wooden floor,' it was imperative that, despite the lack of heat and the high humidity, the artefacts should be shunted back into the Chapel.

The only emergency repository that seemed to offer adequate storage conditions was the National Library of Wales, where, within a few months, problems of a different nature would render the location untenable. Meanwhile the Office of Works admitted that:

> *We may have fallen behind in dealing with repositories scattered through the less accessible areas of the country. But inevitably we must rely on museum representatives to draw attention to anything being overlooked. We understand that the occurrence of any extreme conditions is disastrous for the preservation of your treasures and we are anxious in these matters to provide whatever conditions are regarded as necessary by your representatives.*

At the end of January Dr Plenderleith, the British Museum's chief scientific officer, was despatched to Drayton House to advise on methods of rendering the Chapel and other disused areas of the house suitable for storage. Upon arrival he found the British Museum organization there in utter disarray. Not only were climatic conditions within the house intolerable, but the administrative structure had also collapsed. The problem had arisen on 21 January when Major Stopford-Sackville was recalled to the Service and his family thereupon decided to vacate the house. The family servants were withdrawn and management of the entire house devolved upon a very unwilling British Museum staff. This was a novel situation and one with which the inexperienced personnel at Drayton could not cope. Suddenly they were responsible not only for the museum artefacts but also for the safety of Stopford-Sackville's own possessions, of which an inventory had to be quickly prepared, and for the day-to-day running and maintenance of the estate. E.S. Robinson, the museum's Deputy Keeper of Medals, argued that given the poor conditions at Drayton House and the difficult circumstances staff there found themselves in, it would be best if alternative accommodation could be found. The counter-argument was that with the Stopford-Sackvilles out of the way the museum could extend itself over much more of the house. What troubled the museum staff most, however, was that, following withdrawal of the family servants, they were forced to fend for themselves, something for which they exhibited a marked incapacity. Writing to Sir John Forsdyke outlining his proposals for abandoning

Drayton House, Robinson confided:

I regret that it is necessary, but we now have no Sackville servants at Drayton capable of 'servicing' the British Museum staff. I did not anticipate that the situation would develop as rapidly as it has, but since we are virtually staffless ourselves, I think the change proposed is inevitable.

By the Spring of 1940, as a consequence of the Blitz and the fear of invasion, the safety of the nation's art treasures was radically reassessed. Sir John Forsdyke's ideas for deep underground storage were reconsidered, but little progress was made because, after a preliminary investigation, it appeared that all the available underground accommodation had already been appropriated by the service and supply departments. Forsdyke, however, was confident that, given sufficient application, a solution would be found and in expectation of this many of the proposed removals from one unsuitable country house to another were put on hold.

Thus, Drayton House was temporarily retained and continued to cause trouble. In June rumour reached the Office of Works that the Army intended to billet soldiers in Drayton House and also probably at Boughton. Eric de Normann wrote indignantly to Maurice Wingfield at the War Office to complain. His main fear was that the British soldier's prodigious appetite for cigarettes would entail an unacceptable fire risk. Forsdyke adopted a more sanguine view, welcoming the soldiers because, in his opinion, 'it is good to have them there as a security against possible parachute invaders.' Later the rumours were found to be substantially unfounded; soldiers were not to occupy the houses, but the grounds at Boughton were used for a short while for training.

With improving weather things settled down at Drayton through the summer of 1940, but in September another crisis emerged when, due to recent intensive air raids on London, Major Stopford-Sackville's mother closed up her house in Belgravia and resolved henceforth to live at Drayton House more or less permanently, thus making it extremely difficult to expand the museum accommodation there. On 25 September the museum authorities received notice from Messrs Fisher Saunder & Co., the Stopford-Sackville's agent, that they would be permitted to remain at Drayton House if they could concentrate their artefacts in one large chamber, the King's Dining Room. Three specific conditions were attached to this offer:

1. Ministry of Works engineers must certify that the floor was strong enough to carry the load.
2. The entire floor was to be covered by a protective material.
3. The family's own treasures must be stored in absolute safety elsewhere.

The Office of Works replied that whereas the engineering works presented no problems, 'responsibility for the safe keeping of the Sackville's treasures cannot be accepted by the Department.' The last requirement was subsequently withdrawn but relations with the Stopford-Sackvilles were soured and thereafter somewhat strained.

Despite the manifold difficulties, the British Museum remained in residence at Drayton throughout 1941 but as September drew to a close it became increasingly likely that a centralized underground repository would be available shortly. A disused stone quarry at Westwood in Wiltshire had been identified earlier in the year and it had been thought that conversion of this to make it suitable for the museums would be finished by midsummer. Numerous engineering difficulties delayed its completion, but on 25 September Major Stopford-Sackville heard rumour of its existence, and wrote pleadingly to Bennitt at the Office of Works that he

> *understood that alternative arrangements had been made for the storage of items currently at Drayton and wished to offer the house for similar alternative arrangements for the duration of the war. I should of course be very pleased to think that the house was to remain in the hands of your Ministry for the duration.*

Stopford-Sackville's motivation for this offer may well have been that he was already aware that the Air Ministry had put in a claim for his house as a Service headquarters, an option that was little better than the prospect of evacuee children. Bennitt gave little reassurance, suggesting that continued use of the house as an arts repository depended upon 'the success of a scheme to get private owners and some public bodies who possess works of art to remove them from London.' For a while it appeared that the Soane Museum might be interested in Drayton House, but this plan did not materialize. In April the British Museum gave notice that it would shortly be moving out of both Boughton and Drayton. Arrangements had been made for part of the Science Museum collection to move into Boughton, but Drayton was to be given up to the Air Ministry, much to the chagrin of Stopford-Sackville. In a final attempt to keep his house out of military hands he suggested that the Office of Works might retain possession of at least part of it, writing to Bennitt that:

> *As far as I am concerned, I should resist any attempt of the Air Ministry to acquire unless there are definite restrictions as to the amount of space required.*

Mr Bennitt, however, was not optimistic, replying:

> *The Air Ministry is short of space in this part of the country, so there is little chance of your house being left free. We have every sympathy with your desire to use it for our purposes but there seems little hope of our retaining the house.*

While planning was under way for the underground repository in Wiltshire to absorb the contents of the by now rather vulnerable country houses, Sir John Forsdyke was also canvassing for the abandonment of those sections of the London tube tunnels which were currently used by the British Museum, the Tate Gallery and the V&A. In January 1941, following an engineers' inspection of Aldwych, he informed the Office of Works that:

> The impression I have found from the reports on the Aldwych and Piccadilly tubes is that if suitable underground storage could be found outside London it would be much safer. It appears that should the tubes be hit with bombs larger than 1,000lbs there would probably be serious damage. The tubes are not to be regarded as safe enough to house irreplaceable objects.

British Museum artefacts evacuated to a disused passageway in the Piccadilly Circus tube station.

Skipton Castle, The British Museum's Yorkshire repository.

Towards the end of March the museums were compelled to give up much of the Aldwych tube as a result of pressure applied by Brompton Borough Council which, bowing to press publicity, found itself called upon to acquire at least a part of the tunnel for use as a public air raid shelter. New partition walls erected in connection with the air raid shelters impeded the flow of air around the station tunnels sufficiently to produce a detrimental effect upon the conditions of the stored museum artefacts. Shortly afterwards it was decided to move all the British Museum library material from Aldwych to Skipton Castle in Yorkshire.

A much larger scale and more hazardous move was imminent as a result of an Air Ministry report which stated that west Wales could no longer be considered a safe area as it was now at risk from German bombers flying from northern France. Informing the Office of Works of his intentions, Sir John wrote:

> *You will see that in view of what the Air Ministry says we are bound to move the Aberystwyth things, and there is nowhere else to put them. The proposed Corsham repository is too far away in time and is not yet a practical proposition. I can also say that we shall continue to use Skipton Castle when Corsham is available.*

5

THE VICTORIA & ALBERT MUSEUM

Despite the efforts of Lord Ilchester to discredit it in favour of his own home at Melbury Court, Montacute House near Yeovil in Somerset was selected as the Victoria & Albert Museum's wartime repository on 24 September 1938. Two other west country houses, Langford Court and Sherborne Castle in Dorset, were investigated but rejected for one reason or another. Montacute House, an Elizabethan mansion bequeathed to the National Trust in 1931, was in poor condition when the Office of Works inspected it in 1938. Uninhabited for nearly fifteen years, it had recently acquired a temporary tenant, but had no running water, gas, electricity or adequate heating. A small private generator and primitive wiring had been installed in the early 'twenties, but this had long fallen into disrepair and the Office of Works considered that the whole house would have to be rewired if it was to be connected to the village supply. Nevertheless, the Long Gallery on the upper floor, 189 feet in length, was considered by Sir Eric Maclagan, Director of the V&A, to be particularly suitable to store the museum's treasures and at first it was this room only for which the Office of Works negotiated a tenancy. A potential problem with Montacute was that an Army searchlight battery had recently been set up in the park and the men operating it were billeted in outbuildings close to the house. Wary of the

Aerial view of Montacute House. The long gallery is immediately below the longest east-west eave of the house and was probably the most vulnerable room in the house to incendiary bombing.

Army's proclivity for expansion and aware of the British Museum's difficulty with No.1 Anti-Aircraft Brigade, Sir Eric wrote tersely to the Office of Works, 'We want at all costs to avoid repetition of the Brompton Road Tube story at Montacute.'

The presence of a sitting tenant at Montacute, and the fact that although in poor condition the building was open to the public for limited periods, caused some difficulties and negotiations with the National Trust continued for several months until a resolution was found. Originally it had been intended that the majority of the museum's artefacts should be stored in the basement bomb-proof chamber at South Kensington and only a limited range of items, principally carpets and tapestries, should be transferred to Montacute. The 'bomb-proof room' was ready for occupation on 2 February 1939 but some time before that, as an interim measure, certain items were given special protection where they stood; the Raphael cartoons, for example, were protected by a steel and asbestos curtain. Some items of particular importance that were considered unsuitable for the Kensington basement were sent to West Wycombe Park early in July 1939 as an emergency measure before Montacute was ready, but these were subsequently sent down to Somerset on 29 August, much to the distress of Lady Dashwood who saw their presence at West Wycombe as a guarantee against less amenable house guests. Meanwhile the V&A was approached by the India Office, the Chelsea Royal Hospital and several other institutions with requests that the museum take charge of their most valuable possessions for the duration of the war. In the light of these requests the museum's entire strategy was reassessed and it was decided that Montacute should play a much larger role than originally conceived. On 13 September a new agreement was reached by which the V&A would take over the whole house, buying out the lease of the sitting tenant, cancelling the arrangements by which the house remained open to the public and compensating the National Trust for the consequent loss of income. Two weeks later on 28 September the Office of Works agreed to lease the house on behalf of the V&A for a fee of £450 per annum.

By 4 September, two days after the outbreak of war, the entire contents of the Victoria & Albert Mseum had been evacuated to places of safety, either entombed in the supposedly bomb-proof basement or far away in the west country, free from the risk of enemy bombing. Among the inventory at Montacute were 120 of the museum's best carpets including the priceless indigo silk and wool carpet from the Mosque of Ardabil in Azerbaijan, dating from 1540. Also among the early arrivals at Montacute were sixty tapestries belonging to the museum and a further seventeen that were on loan and on display at Kensington at the outbreak of war, 5590 prints and watercolours, all of the Salting bequest of fifteenth and sixteenth century Italian furniture and the John Jones bequest of eighteenth century French furniture.

Artefacts from the Victoria & Albert Museum being hastily prepared for despatch to the relative safety of Montacute House in September 1939.

Under the original plan it had been intended that the V&A hoard should be packed quite densely in the Long Gallery. Having subsequently taken over the whole house, and despite the fact that the evacuation to Somerset was supposed to have been undertaken beneath a veil of secrecy, the V&A's head custodian at Montacute, Miss Muriel Clayton, the museum's Keeper of Watercolours, suggested that rather than just stack the exhibits away in the house they may as well be laid out in room-sets. It was then suggested that, having gone that far, it might even be possible to allow the public in at 6d (2½p) per visitor. Justifying this proposition, she advised the Trustees that:

> *It is true that a great pretence of secrecy has been observed with regard the place to which the nation's treasures have been sent. But I need hardly tell you that everyone in the neighbourhood knows that our stuff is at Montacute, and I have no doubt that the same applies to the Country Houses that are being used by the British Museum and other national museums and galleries.*

There followed a prolonged and largely irrelevant debate about the security implications of allowing public access (which was largely discounted), and about the contractual difficulties that might arise from the National Trust lease. Eventually, as something of a face-saving compromise, it was decided that casual visitors would not be encouraged but that the V&A would allow visits by serving officers and their wives (but not other family members), by invitation or

41

appointment only.

Things went well at Montacute until the mid-summer of 1940 when Sir Eric Maclagan had to contact his paymasters, the Board of Education, to advise that moths had got into the tapestries at Montacute and that a serious problem was developing. Because of the storage conditions there it was difficult to treat the infected materials without possibly contaminating other exhibits with the powerful insecticide they intended to use. With a marked lack of entomologists among their number, the Board had no useful suggestions to make and on 2 June one of their number, Mr M.G. Holmes, replied pithily:

I'm sorry that at Montacute
The moth's at work with teeth acute,
But if your people work with zest
They'll soon eliminate the pest.

It proved, however, impossible completely to eliminate the pest although constant vigilance kept the worst evils at bay. At all the country house repositories used by the various museums and galleries problems developed with many of the exhibits resulting from the incipient 'shelter-mentality' that tended to overtake the staff under wartime conditions. It was not at first appreciated that the changed circumstances under which most of the artefacts were stored would continue in the long term. When much of the material was packed for despatch it was done so with customary care, but only in a manner that was suitable for the short period that the goods were in transit. At the repositories there was a general feeling of impermanence, that the war would be over by Christmas and the treasures would be quickly returned. This atmosphere, together with the relative shortage of storage space, resulted in many of the exhibits remaining in their transit cases much longer than had been anticipated. While this was of little consequence for many classes of artefact, for others it had severely detrimental consequences. Most of the V&A watercolours, for example, had been packed several dozen to a box, separated by tissue, and after arrival at Montacute remained in their boxes for several months. It was then discovered that the hygroscopic tissue had absorbed atmospheric moisture that was doing considerable damage to the paintings. Thereafter it was realized that the role of such places as Montacute, Boughton House and the rest had to be more than just safe houses; the work of restoration and preservation had to go on more or less as usual to ensure the continued safety of the exhibits. Provision was made for all the manuscripts, prints and pictures at Montacute to be taken from their boxes and frequently aired and examined according to a strict programme. Similarly, bundled textiles were opened up and all the carpets and tapestries were regularly unrolled and minutely examined.

Staff at Montacute, like their counterparts at Boughton and elsewhere, felt that as a result of insidious Treasury influence the drive for economy at the country house repositories, particularly in respect of fuel for heating, was working to the detriment of the artefacts stored there. Sir Eric Maclagan's opinion was that:

> *Where those objects concerned are National Property of vast historical importance and of immense value, I venture to suggest that the rigid economy with which the collections are housed and maintained at Montacute is an unsound policy, and that no reasonable additional expenditure, which would ensure them from deterioration, should be grudged.*

By the autumn of 1940, with the German air force occupying aerodromes throughout northern France, none of the southern counties of England could be considered secure from enemy bombing and Montacute was no longer any safer than South Kensington. Although the greatest risk was from incendiary bombs, the Office of Works was inordinately worried about the increasing number of British soldiers camped in the grounds of the house, whom they seemed to consider, with their apparently insatiable appetite for cheap cigarettes, as no more than a horde of latent arsonists.

It was felt that the Long Gallery at Montacute presented a particularly dangerous fire risk as the heavily timbered roof space was inaccessible from below and could only be reached by a tortuous route across steeply sloping roofs and thence through a couple of skylights. It was

Interior view of the Long Gallery at Montacute.

subsequently agreed with the National Trust that three hatches should be cut in the ceiling of the gallery and portable, wheeled ladders provided to gain access to them. Montacute was also considered a difficult house to evacuate items from in the event of fire. The small fixed windows on the upper floor prevented salvage by the recognized and aptly named 'tipping' technique, which simply involved tipping rescued material out of the nearest available opening, and the narrow, convoluted corridors hindered the rapid evacuation of large items of furniture. Consideration had to be given to the immediate fate of the museum artefacts following a serious fire at the house as it was obvious that they could not be left piled on the lawns. Staff calculated that within the house the exhibits occupied some 12,000 square feet, but that in emergency this could be compacted into rather less than half that space. During the winter of 1940/1 a search of the estate and nearby villages was instituted for outbuildings suitable for use as 'domestic base hospitals' or temporary stores for use in such an emergency. Disquiet about the suitability of Montacute House increased throughout the winter as the bombing intensified and there was much talk of moving, at the very least, the museum's book collection back to the bomb-proof chamber at Kensington.

Following discussions between Sir Eric Maclagan, Sir John Forsdyke and Sir Patrick Duff in March 1941 it became apparent that the Office of Works had been in negotiation for some weeks past into the possibility of providing absolutely secure underground protection in the Corsham area. An over-optimistic prediction that this capacity might be available as early as June relieved much of the pressure on both the V&A at Montacute and the various country houses currently offering dubious sanctuary to the British Museum. In fact, another year was to elapse before the Westwood Quarry near Corsham was ready for occupation, by which time German air activity had diminished to almost negligible levels and the threat of invasion had evaporated.

6

WESTWOOD QUARRY

Historically, the Office of Works had been a very small organization with few responsibilities beyond the maintenance of certain Crown properties and ancient monuments. The Second World War, however, saw an enormous expansion of its remit and one that it was not fully qualified to undertake. Lacking personnel in both number, experience and ability, it was continuously punching above its weight with the result that many of the projects it was involved with progressed inefficiently and were often bogged down by bureaucracy. Sensitive of its own weakness and suspicious that it was often sidelined on major issues in which it should be involved, the department quickly gained a reputation for excessive intrusiveness in its effort to take control of projects that bolstered its own credibility. With regard to the evacuation of art treasures, the Office of Works considered that the entire process should be under its control and was incensed by the prospect of individual museums and galleries making independent provisions.

Towards the end of March 1939, in response to Sir John Forsdyke's widely heard call for underground storage as a more secure alternative to the Country House scheme, Eric de Normann questioned Sir Eric Maclagan, hoping to elicit more details about the surreptitious arrangements for the evacuation of art treasures that he suspected were being prepared by the British Museum and the National Gallery. Maclagan, who at that time knew little more than had been circulated at meetings of the Museums and Galleries ARP Committee, replied that:

I have no really official information about the plan for the National Gallery and British Museum except that their objects are to go to Wales and that, as I understand, Aberystwyth University is to be used as a sort of distribution centre. But I have heard stories about really elaborate precautions for a place of almost absolute security in the Welsh Mountains.

Perturbed by this, de Normann made further enquiries and two days later informed Maclagan that:

All that it amounts to in fact, as far as I know, is a comparatively small tunnel under the National Museum of Wales at Aberystwyth. The British Museum have part-user, and the National Gallery are using some of the Library itself. Forsdyke is shortly visiting a salt mine in Cheshire and it is possible that something may come of that.

In fact, both the British Museum and the National Gallery had been following the underground route quite independently for some months. The National Gallery's motivation was twofold; first, in response to

45

recent Air Ministry warnings the Trustees were keen to vacate the now somewhat vulnerable buildings they occupied on the west Wales coast, and secondly they were desperate to rid themselves of Lord Penrhyn, their unwilling host at Penrhyn Castle. For the British Museum, Sir John Forsdyke had from the earliest days made plain his opinion that underground storage was the only safe refuge in war. His discovery of Westwood Quarry near Bradford-on-Avon in Wiltshire was fortuitous and came about as a result of a chance meeting with W. L. Cooper, the Chief Librarian of the University of Bristol. Cooper had arranged at the very start of the war to secrete most of the university's extensive collection of medieval books and manuscripts in a small, disused stone quarry at Elm Park, some two miles south-east of Corsham in Wiltshire. Cooper became aware of the quarry through his association with Mark Pictor, chairman of the Bath and Portland Stone Company, from whom the University had purchased large quantities of stone in the immediate pre-war years for an extensive restoration and expansion programme. Throughout most of the war the larger part of Elm Park Quarry was used by the RAF as a bomb store, with the university occupying just one small and very damp heading. Stone quarries in the Corsham area of north Wiltshire played a pivotal role in many aspects of the war, many kept secret for decades after the defeat of Germany, and it is perhaps worth investigating these briefly before looking in more detail at Westwood.

During the century prior to 1934 the quarrymen of north Wiltshire had extracted building stone of the finest quality from mineral reserves one hundred feet below the villages of Box and Corsham. As they progressed they left behind a ramified network of worked-out chambers and galleries that extended, under Corsham Down alone, to some three thousand acres. It was said that one could walk in a straight line underground from the edge of Box Hill to Pockeredge Farm near the eastern portal of Box railway tunnel, a distance of over two miles, without seeing daylight. The construction of Box Tunnel by the Great Western Railway in 1838 had exposed the vast reserves of oolitic limestone under Corsham Down, and the largest of the quarries was subsequently developed close by. Directly to the north, Tunnel and Huddswell quarries sprawled over two million square feet and came to within twenty feet of the tunnel lining. Immediately to the south lay Spring Quarry, even larger at 3,500,000 square feet. By 1934 the stone industry was in terminal decline, Tunnel Quarry had been abandoned six years earlier while Spring Quarry was nearing the end of its reserves and was only marginally profitable.

Early in 1934 Tunnel Quarry was purchased by the War Office and over the next six years was converted into a huge underground ammunition depot designed to store the entire war reserves of ammunition for the British land forces. At an early stage in the Tunnel Quarry project, the Army Council minuted to the Treasury that:

It is a programme which may cost £100,000 or £250,000, or £500,000
according to the amount of work which must be done. Whatever is the case
it is not open to us to be content with anything less.

As the project progressed it became apparent that even the largest of
these estimates was hopelessly optimistic and would represent just a tiny
fraction of the true final cost which was in excess of £4.4 million.

It was, then, with considerable alarm that the Treasury learned in
December 1940 that, under pressure from Lord Beaverbrook, the
Minister of Aircraft Production, Churchill had been persuaded to
sanction the conversion of Spring Quarry into the largest underground
factory in the world, producing Centaurus radial engines for the Bristol
Aeroplane Company.

Whereas the Corsham ammunition depot had been built under the
close control of the War Office, the underground factory scheme was
immediately hijacked by the Ministry of Works and Buildings (the old
Office of Works renamed to reflect its enlarged role and irreverently
called the 'Ministry of Works and Bricks' by its employees). Under the
MOWB the factory scheme leapfrogged in magnitude; not just Spring
Quarry, but every quarry owned by the Bath and Portland Stone
Company within a twenty mile radius of Corsham was peremptorily
requisitioned and plans prepared for its conversion into a factory of
some kind or another for as yet unidentified tenants. Shocked by the
requisitioning of all his property, which marked the immediate end of
the quarrying industry in Wiltshire and the loss of several hundred jobs,
Mark Pictor, Chairman of the company, wrote to his land agent on
Monday 2 December 1940:

> *On Saturday the District Valuer arrived at our office and requisitioned the*
> *whole of our Bath Stone quarries with the exception of Monk's Park,*
> *which had been requisitioned a few days earlier by the Admiralty. This has*
> *come as rather a surprise to us as we did not anticipate the Ministry of*
> *Supply stepping in at all.*
>
> *No question of terms was discussed as he said that would be dealt with*
> *later. I tried to find out whether we should be allowed to do the clearing*
> *but could get no reply on that point. As you can imagine we are left rather*
> *high and dry, but I suppose we shall hear something this week.*
>
> *Meantime of course it is somewhat difficult to know what to do with the*
> *men as I do not want to disperse them knowing how difficult it will be to*
> *get them back again, but with all the quarries requisitioned it leaves little*
> *work to which we can put them.*

The underground factory scheme was an ill-conceived panic response to
the intensive German attacks upon the British aircraft industry. Mindful
of the forty-fold increase in cost of the War Office underground depot in
Corsham, a Treasury official noted to his Minister in December 1940,
when the estimated cost of the project had already reached £2,341,000,

that 'I think there is no alternative to sanction the scheme in principal, but to ask that a close watch be kept on development.'

A year later very little work had been completed on site other than the removal of stone debris from underground, but the estimate had passed £6,000,000. Waste removal alone had already absorbed over £2,000,000, prompting the same Treasury official to ask the Minister for Works and Buildings:

> *Quarry development at £2,227,000 looks Pretty Sinister. Is this a repetition of the War Office experience at Corsham? Why have we not been told of this enormous increase of cost at an earlier stage?*

This, however, was only the start of the troubles. The factory was still not ready for occupation by the end of 1942, by which time the German bombing had reduced to insignificance and the whole underground factory scheme had become an irrelevance. No one, other than Beaverbrook, was enthusiastic. Neither the Bristol Aeroplane Company management nor the employees wanted to go underground. The Treasury had been vehemently opposed to the project from the start and the War Office was convinced that development of the factory would prejudice the security of its own underground establishments in the Corsham area. Badly managed, poorly executed, and overshadowed by accusations of profiteering on the part of some of the contractors involved, the Spring Quarry project had acquired an evil reputation and an unstoppable internal momentum. Construction continued despite its patent irrelevance in a manner that defied logical analysis.

The completed factory extended over 2,200,000 square feet of underground space and was divided into three major sections by geological faults. The main offices, workshops, and canteens were concentrated in the larger eastern section which encompassed over half the available area. The west end of the quarry was divided by a second, lateral, fault and provides two smaller areas, each of approximately 500,000 square feet. The southernmost of these was also converted into engineering shops but the northern area was never fully developed. To facilitate the easy movement of some 20,000 employees in and out of the factory each day two inclined shafts were fitted with 'Otis' electric escalators requisitioned from St Paul's and Holborn tube stations in London. These were supplemented by four high-capacity electric passenger lifts in vertical shafts, while a further five heavy-duty lifts were installed to move goods and materials in and out of the quarry. Process steam was provided by two underground boilerhouses each with six large coal-fired boilers, and for the benefit of the employees there were five underground restaurants that could jointly cater for over six thousand diners at a sitting.

By April 1945, when the factory finally closed, the bill for its construction had passed £20,000,000, with half as much again spent on machine tools. Yet it had produced virtually nothing of note except a small number of Centaurus engines, many of which failed at the test stage due to the poor conditions under which they were assembled. The overspend at Spring Quarry was so notorious that it prompted an unprecedented House of Commons Public Accounts Committee enquiry, the only time that such an inquiry had investigated a defence project in wartime.

Several other quarries in the vicinity of Spring Quarry were also developed under the overall umbrella of the Ministry of Aircraft production scheme. Among these was the 720,000 square foot Westwood Quarry, which lies fifteen miles west of Corsham below a precipitous hillside overlooking the incongruous industrial hamlet of Avoncliff in the Avon valley. It is the most remote of all the quarries requisitioned under the Corsham scheme and, once the immediate panic to go underground had subsided, was the first earmarked for abandonment.

Westwood was allocated in an arbitrary manner to the Royal Enfield Company, whose motorcycle factory in Solihull had been adapted early in the war for the making of bomb sights, and which, by 1941, the Ministry of Aircraft Production considered too vulnerable. The Royal Enfield Board was not enthusiastic about the move and their attitude, combined with slow progress on the part of the contractors and a relaxation in German bombing, almost resulted in the abandonment of the project. The MAP, however, was insistent and eventually the factory was occupied although on a smaller scale than at first anticipated. One heading at the extreme innermost end of the quarry was surplus to the

A typical view of the larger, eastern section of the quarry which was converted into an underground factory in 1940.

needs of the Royal Enfield Company and it was this area, extending over 25,000 square feet, that was, after a number of false starts, finally occupied by the London museums.

The minutes of the British Museum Trustees record that as early as February 1940, some ten months before the MOWB stepped in to requisition the quarries, Sir John Forsdyke had been in contact with the Bath and Portland Stone Company with a view to inspecting Westwood. The record notes that:

It is evident that all documents and objects of first-rate national importance ought to be put underground, but efforts made in that direction by the trustees and Ministry of Works have so far been unsuccessful. Arrangements were made some time ago with the Bath Stone Firm at Corsham to inspect a quarry which they offered for storage. But we were stopped the day before our inspection by the Air Ministry who claimed all quarries for their own use, or at least for their consideration. The present position is that all quarries are held up for them. When one is released we can take it if suitable, but construction work, heating and ventilation will be needed and the materials for these are reserved indefinitely for military purposes.

A year later no progress had been achieved, but Maclagan and Forsdyke were now working in concert and, frustrated at the low priority they were receiving in the distribution of all resources in comparison with the Armed Services, they determined to voice their frustration to the Treasury. Early in February 1941, with all the country houses fearfully vulnerable to enemy bombing, Sir John Forsdyke wrote:

It was recognized long before the war by the Museums and Galleries, and by the Office of Works, that the only safe storage would be underground. Accommodation in Tube Railway stations and tunnels was provided in good time, and this is satisfactory as far as it goes, but it does not go very far. The kind of material that can be kept in a tube tunnel is limited to what is waterproof. The humidity of the tubes is normally too high, if electric power is cut off it will rise to saturation point, and even with watertight doors there is a risk of flooding.

For the very much larger mass of perishable material which was selected for evacuation (books, manuscripts, drawings, paintings and objects of art) country repositories were allocated to us according to our needs. Only one of the three, the National Library of Wales, is a strong or fireproof building, and I have just been warned by the Air Ministry to get out of this because its locality has become dangerous. Other locations have been made dangerous by the construction of aerodromes or barracks nearby.

So our repositories are no safer than other country houses, most are isolated, old and inflammable and their protection against fire depends upon the few men we can post there as guards. But they contain in concentrated form the most valuable and most delicate things that the nation possesses. The whole collection of coins and medals, for instance, of which the mere monetary value must be at least three million pounds, is stacked on the floor of the Duke of Buccleuch's kitchens at Boughton.

The tapestries of the V&A are stored in similar conditions at Montacute. Some of the medieval ivories are there, the rest are in the basement at South Kensington and I do not know that one lot is any safer than the other.

It is evident that the perishable things of first-rate importance ought to be put underground. You know that before the war my Trustees pressed for a tunnel in the rock at Aberystwyth and were allowed to spend £3,000 out of savings on it. The loose rock that was discovered doubled the cost of construction and the size of the repository was therefore halved. What we have there is fifty-six feet of tunnel eight feet high and eight feet wide which contains the best of our manuscripts, books, prints and drawings. This is, as far as I know, the only underground repository of its kind, unless the quarry-shelter of the National Gallery at Blaenau Ffestiniog is finished.

The rest of my books and manuscripts, evicted from Aberystwyth, will have to go under a glass roof in the banqueting hall of Skipton Castle. For the prints and drawings I can find no other place and they must take their chances at Aberystwyth.

Some weeks ago I got in touch with the Bath Stone Firm at Corsham and arranged with the Office of Works to inspect a quarry which they offered us for storage. One quarry might give us space enough for the first-line material of all the museums and galleries [the National Gallery being already provided for]. Its lock-up chambers would need little guarding and that could be done by a joint staff.

What we want now is not priority but a moment of parity with the Service Departments. I should not be surprised to hear that nothing can be done, but in that event my letter will have served to ensure that everybody who is interested in the matter knows the facts, and that if we have to announce major disasters among the national collections the news will not be received by the government with surprise.

Writing of the Corsham stone quarries, Sir John described them as being:

as bomb-proof as the salt mines in Cheshire which were offered to us at the beginning of the war by ICI and rejected by us because of problems of humidity, storage and access. These problems would be simple in the stone quarries, new construction would be easy and space has been offered to us there. An objection might be that similar quarries are being used for munitions of war.

A few days later, following a conversation with Sir Kenneth Clark during which he heard the full story of the proposed National Gallery storage facility at Manod in Snowdonia, which had finally received reluctant backing from the Ministry of Works and Buildings, Sir John Forsdyke, piqued that the National Gallery had quite independently achieved what he had unsuccessfully sought for the whole museums organization since the start of the war, demanded of the MOWB:

I am told that you are accommodating the National Gallery in a Welsh quarry; if this is so it would seem that the policy of removal is appropriate for your department. Is there not room for us in the National Gallery quarry?

By the beginning of March the argument was becoming increasingly public and overwhelmingly in support of universal underground protection for works of art. Given that Forsdyke's persistent lobbying had gained the backing of the Prime Minister the MOWB had no option but to give way and on 6 March a meeting was arranged at Westwood Quarry between Sir Eric Maclagan, Sir John Forsdyke, Mr Bennitt from the MOWB and representatives of Sir Alexander Gibb & Partners, the civil engineers in charge of the Corsham quarry project. Plans of the quarry were examined and it was found that the 20,000 square-foot heading identified some eighteen months earlier was available. It was agreed that sufficient space could be provided there to satisfy the needs of the British Museum and the V&A, and the MOWB confirmed that they would be able adequately to air-condition the area.

Westwood Quarry was served by one main entrance tunnel entering from the north; to the east of the tunnel lay the extensive workshops of the Royal Enfield Company and beyond those were several acres of disused workings that had latterly been used for mushroom cultivation. The area proposed for museum storage lay at the southern, innermost, end of the access corridor and an area to the west of this was earmarked as the plant room for standby generators and air-conditioning

A typical view of the old quarry workings at Westwood prior to the wartime development.

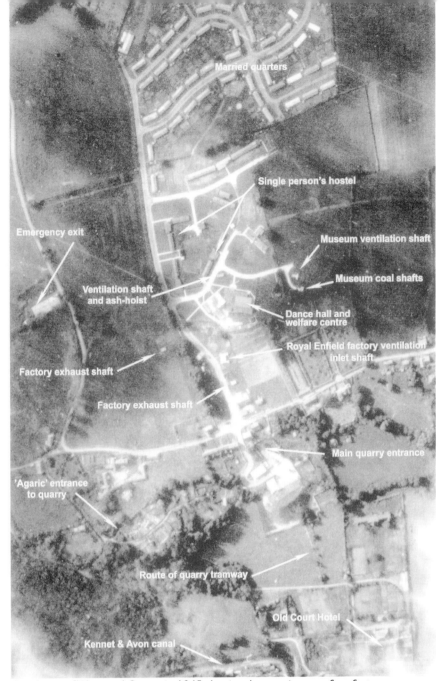

Married quarters

Single person's hostel

Emergency exit

Museum ventilation shaft

Ventilation shaft
and ash-hoist

Museum coal shafts

Dance hall and
welfare centre

Royal Enfield factory ventilation
inlet shaft

Factory exhaust shaft

Factory exhaust shaft

Main quarry entrance

'Agaric' entrance
to quarry

Route of quarry tramway

Old Court Hotel

Kennet & Avon canal

Aerial view of Westwood Quarry in 1945 showing the prominent surface features.

equipment. Unlike the quarries nearer Corsham, Westwood was relatively clear of the waste stone and detritus of the earlier industry, as this had largely been cleared when the site was taken over for mushroom farming in the 1920s. Some preparatory work, too, had been undertaken by the MOWB before the Royal Enfield factory scheme was scaled back, so by March 1941 the amount of development outstanding to achieve the conditions required for the museums was not excessively daunting.

During the 1920s, when quarrying at Westwood was at its peak, there was a serious roof fall along a fault line that traverses the quarry and in consequence a number of suspect pillars were secured with huge chains to prevent any further movement.

To the casual observer immediately before the war, none of the Corsham quarries would have appeared likely candidates for conversion to storage facilities for the nation's treasures, or indeed to factories, ammunition depots or any of the other uses to which they were ultimately put. Dank, dark and dripping with moisture, the floors ankle deep in sloppy, sticky yellow clay, support pillars straining under pressure from the roof and passageways often blocked by roof falls, the quarries looked hardly safe or secure. Four years of labour by twelve thousand men, the majority of them Irish navvies who replaced British labourers progressively called-up to the services, changed all that. Floors were graded, quarry roofs supported by the insertion of steel girders and pillars strengthened where required with reinforced concrete corsets. There were inevitable difficulties and delays: underground construction on this scale was quite novel in the British Isles and there were no experienced contractors to take on the job. Materials were in short supply and as the war dragged on labour difficulties developed, particularly at remote Westwood where the Irishmen demanded parity payments to make up for the benefits their compatriots at the main Corsham site received and they did not.

Sir Alexander Gibb & Partners subcontracted the Westwood job to Wimpey who assured the MOWB that it would be completed in six months, i.e by the end of September 1941, when the museums had been tacitly promised occupation of the quarry. It was agreed that capacity at

Westwood would be divided initially between the V&A, the British Museum and the Public Record Office, and in May Sir Eric Maclagan wrote to Mr Stanton of Alexander Gibb & Co. to outline his requirements. At that time the V&A occupied 12,000 square feet at Montacute and maintained a further 3,000 square feet in the Kensington basement. Maclagan informed Stanton that:

> It is difficult to estimate the amount of space that would be required for the most valuable objects still in the V&A since they are packed very closely on steel shelves in a quite small chamber in the basement which has been made as nearly bomb-proof as possible.

Gibb's produced two estimates for quarry conversion; the first was for the development of 13,000 square feet solely for the V&A, at a cost of £13,000 and the second for 23,000 square feet to be shared between the museums at a cost of £19,500. The latter proposal, with amendments, was finally accepted.

The floor of the quarry sloped markedly at a gradient of 1:30 and while this presented little problem to the British Museum, the bulk of whose artefacts were securely boxed and could be stacked on shelving with a small ground footprint, but, Sir Eric Maclagan advised,

> The Victoria & Albert has a good deal of antique furniture which must stand on level floors, and about one third of its accommodation (say 5,000 square feet) should be thus prepared.

A general view of the quarry showing part of the V&A furniture collection on the left and library material from the British Museum in racks on the right.

The east (Victoria & Albert) side of the quarry shortly after the completion of building work, showing the stepped floor alllowing large items of furniture to be stacked on the level.

Rolled carpets and textiles stored in Westwood quarry.

Measures were put in hand to terrace the upper half of the left-hand side of the quarry (which had already been allocated to the V&A) to provide this. The average roof height was seven to eight feet. The V&A further specified that the minimum entrance width to the quarry should be not less than four feet, and that within the repository there should be a twenty-foot clear run to enable the largest rolled carpets to be manoeuvred. There was also to be a clear area forty-five feet by twenty-five feet to allow the large carpets to be periodically unrolled for inspection.

When Sir John Forsdyke visited the quarry on 26 June he found a disappointing state of affairs. Reporting to the Board of Education, he wrote:

> You asked me to let you know about the progress of the scheme for the quarry repository which the Archbishop put to the Prime Minister last February. Arrangements have been put in hand and were going well, but latterly there has been some hold up, possibly Treasury, or possibly Service Department interference. The Engineers are ready and waiting, but the only activity is some architectural ornamentation of the entrance tunnel by a few stonemasons.

Substantial work resumed on 16 July and it was planned that this should be implemented in three stages. The third of the quarry furthest from the entrance should be completed first, and the third nearest the entrance, which included the inspection room and offices, was to be completed last.

Gangers emerging from Westwood quarry in 1896. The young man in a white cap, second from the right on the back of the stone blocks, is the man sitting on the front of the foremost electric truck in the 1944 photograph of the quarry entrance on the following page.

Reconstruction of the quarry entrance nears completion in 1943. Note the narrow-gauge railway tracks used during construction. This system was retained for a short while by the museums for transporting their artefacts underground but was subsequently replaced by a small fleet of electric trucks.

Below the completed entrance portal in 1944.

Staff leaving the quarry, 1944.

Despite the setbacks the museum directors were still confident that they would be able to move into the quarry by the end of September. Early in August the logistics of the move were being addressed and there was some concern about finding suitable billets for the evacuated museum staff. Most of the available accommodation in the Bath and Corsham areas had already been taken up by Service personnel, dispersed factory workers employed in the underground factories and Admiralty staff who had been evacuated to Bath in 1939. On 29 August Mr Bennitt of the MOWB was sent down to investigate progress at Westwood Quarry and to look into the housing problem. Sir John Forsdyke sent Bennitt, who had never visited the quarry before, a map of the immediate area, noting:

> *I have marked with a red cross the entrance to our quarry and have also marked in red the hotel (formerly a workhouse) at which I expect you will be entertained by Sir Alexander Gibb & Partners, and at which I hope to get my officers billeted.*

The hotel to which Sir John referred was *The Old Court* at Avoncliff in the Avon valley a couple of hundred yards below the quarry entrance. The curiously shaped early Georgian building was built as an apprentice house for a nearby woollen mill but fell into disuse at the turn of the nineteenth century. In 1834 it became the Bradford Union Workhouse under the *Poor Law Amendment Act* of that year. Sir John was ultimately

Built as apprentice housing for a nearby woollen mill and subsequently used, after 1834, as the Bradford Union workhouse, this range of early Georgian buildings had, by 1939, become the Old Court Hotel. It was requisitioned in 1942 for use as the wartime administrative headquarters of the British Museum.

successful in having his officers billeted there and by the end of 1942 the entire building was in the possession of the British Museum and it had become, for the duration of the war, the museum's administrative headquarters. Letters from the museum in those years were written on headed notepaper with its London address 'Bloomsbury' crossed out and overstamped 'Avoncliff'. Such letters will perhaps mark Avoncliff's place in history, recording that for five years one of the smallest hamlets in Britain was host to one of the most important museums in the world.

While the problem of accommodating the chief officers of the museum was resolved by the acquisition of the *Old Court Hotel*, finding homes for the rest of the staff was not. Sir John pressed the Ministry of Works and Buildings to allow his men to occupy part of the working men's

Because in wintertime, workers underground at Westwood would rarely be exposed to daylight, all staff were required to undertake one hour of compulsory ultra-violet light treatment each week.

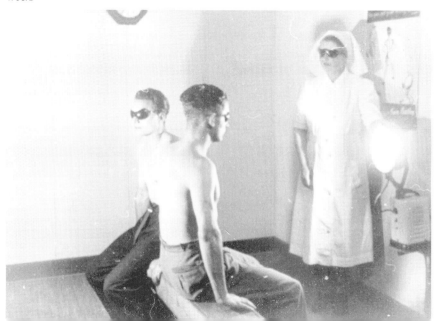

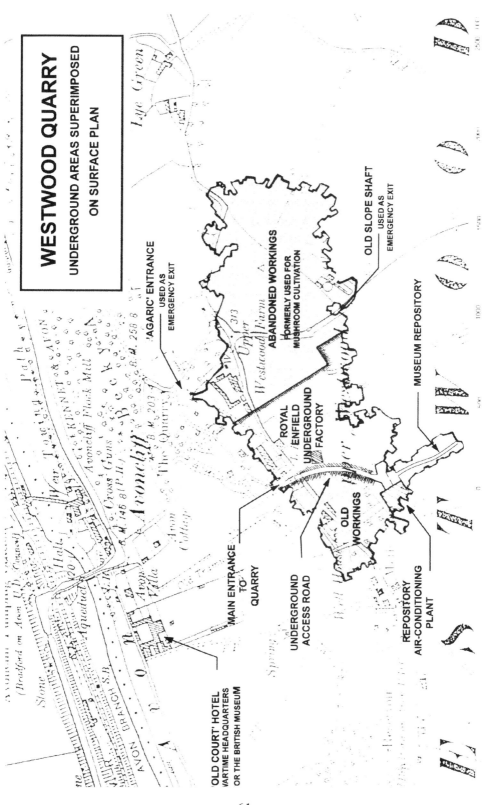

WESTWOOD QUARRY
UNDERGROUND AREAS SUPERIMPOSED
ON SURFACE PLAN

'AGARIC' ENTRANCE
USED AS
EMERGENCY EXIT

ABANDONED WORKINGS
FORMERLY USED FOR
MUSHROOM CULTIVATION

OLD SLOPE SHAFT
USED AS
EMERGENCY EXIT

ROYAL
ENFIELD
UNDERGROUND
FACTORY

MUSEUM REPOSITORY

OLD
WORKINGS

MAIN ENTRANCE
TO
QUARRY

UNDERGROUND
ACCESS ROAD

REPOSITORY
AIR-CONDITIONING
PLANT

'OLD COURT' HOTEL
WARTIME HEADQUARTERS
OR THE BRITISH MUSEUM

61

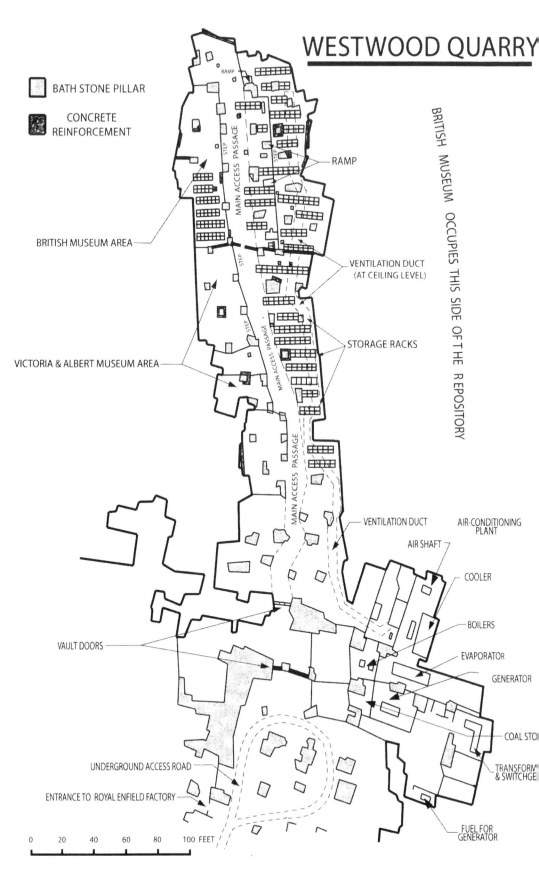

WESTWOOD QUARRY

BATH STONE PILLAR

CONCRETE REINFORCEMENT

RAMP

BRITISH MUSEUM AREA

MAIN ACCESS PASSAGE

STEP

STEP

STEP

BRITISH MUSEUM OCCUPIES THIS SIDE OF THE REPOSITORY

VENTILATION DUCT
(AT CEILING LEVEL)

STORAGE RACKS

VICTORIA & ALBERT MUSEUM AREA

MAIN ACCESS PASSAGE

MAIN ACCESS PASSAGE

VENTILATION DUCT

AIR-CONDITIONING
PLANT

AIR SHAFT

COOLER

BOILERS

EVAPORATOR

GENERATOR

VAULT DOORS

COAL STO

TRANSFORM
& SWITCHGE

UNDERGROUND ACCESS ROAD

ENTRANCE TO ROYAL ENFIELD FACTORY

FUEL FOR
GENERATOR

0   20   40   60   80   100 FEET

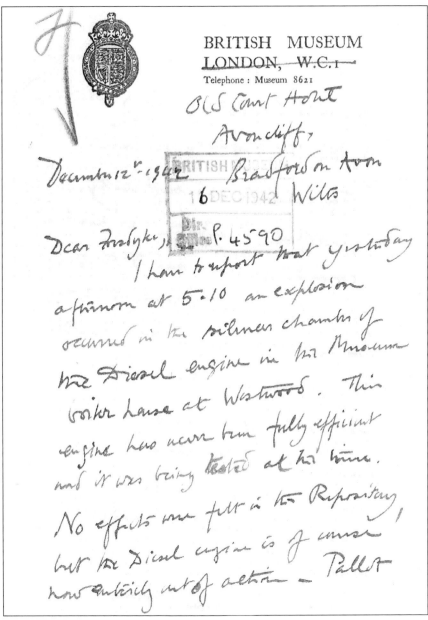

BRITISH MUSEUM
LONDON, W.C.1
Telephone : Museum 8621

Old Court Hotel

Avoncliff,

December 12th 1942   Bradford on Avon

16 DEC 1942   Wilts

P. 4590

Dear Forsdyke,
I have to report that yesterday afternoon at 5.10 an explosion occurred in the silencer chamber of the Diesel engine in the Museum boiler house at Westwood. This engine has never been fully efficient and it was being tested at the time. No effects were felt in the Repository, but the Diesel engine is of course now entirely out of action — Pallot

This letter, dated 12 December 1942, from the Old Court Hotel at Avoncliff, is the first intimation of the troubles to come at Westwood.

hostel and some of the wooden huts that served as married quarters built to house workers employed in the underground factory. He also asked for them to be allowed to use the workmen's canteen, worrying that 'otherwise I really do not see how our people are to get any food or drink.'

Up until the summer of 1941 the existence of the Westwood repository was a closely guarded secret and few people outside of the Ministry of Works and Buildings other than Sir Eric Maglagan and Sir John Forsdyke were aware of the work going on there. However, the time was approaching when the custodians at the various country house repositories would have to be told to make ready for the move. Writing to Muriel Clayton at Montacute asking her to begin preparations for the long-awaited move to a secret underground location, Sir John stated:

I am not at liberty at present to tell you where the quarry is, but it is in the West of England and no more than forty miles from Montacute as the crow flies.

Rather to Sir John's surprise, Miss Clayton replied:

I read your letter about the quarry with the greatest interest. Incidentally, I had already heard of the scheme through the medium of one of the less-reputable daily papers, which had a paragraph a couple of months ago about 'art treasures in the caves', stating that several of the great museums were proposing to take shelter in disused mine workings.

Muriel Clayton was not convinced that concentrating all the nation's art treasures in one location was wise and had always argued that dispersal was the best policy. She suggested, for example, that the majority of the furniture should remain at Montacute and that of the nation's six 'Triumph' tapestries, the three at Hampton Court Palace should remain there, two of the three in the V&A collection currently at Montacute should remain and the third should go underground. Referring to other items in the collection, she stated:

I have discussed it with Edwards of 'Woodwork' who agrees that the bulk of the furniture must stay where it is. He thinks also that the caskets and boxed objects might go. If it is possible I should like most of the Opus Anglicanum [the V&A collection of C13th Church Embroidery] now in the Bomb-Proof to depart.

Miss Clayton's principal concern was the risk of moth infestation at both

Textiles from the British Museum's ethnographic department were stored within a separate chamber in the quarry in order that the chemicals used in the programme of insecticide spraying would not damage other artefacts.

This is the outer vault door which, like the larger inner door, is still used by Wansdyke Security Ltd., the current operators of the repository. These doors have in recent years been supplemented by a modern Chubb door with multi-point locking bolts.

the quarry and at Montacute. It was her opinion that while the risk was higher at Montacute the facilities for subsequent treatment there were much better as there was more space and less risk of chemical contamination of other artefacts. By August, however, it had been decided that the whole contents of the Kensington basement and virtually all the items at Montacute except some Library material, a few carpets of mediocre quality and fifteen boxes of textiles would be transferred to Westwood.

Preparations for the transfer were well under way in August and thought was being given to the physical security of the site. Forsdyke asked the MOWB whether it intended to provide safe-type doors at the entrance to the repository, commenting that just in case it was not he

A view from the outer vault door of the repository looking down the main access tunnel towards the quarry entrance.

had already arranged for the removal of two such doors from the British Museum vaults at Bloomsbury. One was seven feet six inches high and six feet wide, the other four feet five inches wide and nine feet three inches high and it was intended that this should be the inner-most door of the entrance air-lock. Forsdyke acknowledged that the larger door was somewhat taller than the quarry headroom would allow, but thought it would not be difficult to hack out a recess in the roof to accommodate it.

Meanwhile the schedule by which the V&A artefacts would be evacuated from the existing repositories was decided. First to go would be the Dyce manuscripts, the notebooks of Leonardo da Vinci and Shakespeare's first folio, followed by the Dickens manuscripts and the museum's collection of medieval illuminated manuscripts. These would be followed by items from the Salting and Currie bequests. The most important artefacts still retained in the bomb-proof room in Kensington would be given first priority, followed by the best items from Montacute and then the remaining balance from Montacute.

On 8 September, with the anticipated removal day little more than three weeks away, inspectors from the V&A again visited Westwood to gauge the progress of the work. Upon arrival they found the quarry in a sorry state with basic building work months behind schedule and new problems arising daily. They were promised by Gibb's representative at Westwood that the situation was now under control and that the site would be ready for handover at the end of November. One of the problems was that the complex air-conditioning plant specified by the MOWB had not yet arrived on site and installation could not begin until 30 October. Because of the dimensions of the plant, the huge strong-room doors from Bloomsbury could not be erected until the air-conditioning equipment had been fixed in place. Elsewhere things were more advanced. Within the repository the floors were finished and men were at work applying 'Sica' damp-proofing agent to the walls. Outside, narrow gauge rails were laid in the entrance tunnel and out into the yard where a lifting gantry was erected to unload crates from the lorries as they arrived.

It was realized from the outset that very careful control over the temperature and humidity would be required, and a contract to supply plant capable of maintaining a temperature of 65° and relative humidity of sixty per cent was awarded to the Norris Warming Company. The installed equipment was very sophisticated and very extensive, requiring a plant room almost as large as the repository it served. Much of the plant was duplicated, for it was calculated that should it fail for more than thirty minutes or so conditions would deteriorate so rapidly that the more delicate items in storage would suffer irreparable damage. Experimental

The chilled-water dehumidifier, installed by the Norris Warming Company in 1942 and still in reasonable condition sixty years later.

Two coal-fired boilers in the underground boilerhouse at Westwood. Fuel was tipped down a pair of vertical shafts from a small yard on the surface, and waste ashes were disposed of by means of a chain-hoist and drum in a dedicated shaft.

'Cambridge' humidity recorders continuously monitored atmospheric conditions in the repository, but adjustment of the plant was performed manually and required great vigilance from the plant attendants. Within the storage chambers men were employed whose sole job was constantly to inspect the walls and floor for signs of damp. When found these were treated with 'Stett', a proprietary damp proofing compound.

Following the initial delay in delivery, the plant was erected in just ten days and first run on 10 November 1941. The results, however, were not promising; after two weeks continuous operation there was no measurable change in the humidity level and high-powered portable dehumidifiers were brought in to help reduce the initial levels to something more manageable. Thereafter the situation slowly improved but the MOWB was compelled to notify the museums that a further three months would be required to dry the quarry adequately. In the meantime it was found that while the plant, running at full power, could just maintain a relative humidity of sixty five per cent, if it was stopped for just a few minutes the humidity rose immediately to ninety per cent.

Towards the end of February 1942 a state of equilibrium was achieved, final tests were conducted and on 17 March Mr Bennitt from the MOWB advised Sir Eric Maclagan that:

> I am directed by the Ministry of Works and Buildings to inform you that the quarry which has been adapted for storing museum treasures at Westwood near Bath is now complete, subject to minor points of adjustment which will be discussed with your officers locally. Arrangements may, therefore, be made to move your treasures in.

A rota was organized by which artefacts from the British Museum and the V&A arrived on alternate days. All movements of V&A materials were by lorry and the packing and handling was undertaken by expert V&A staff under the guidance of Mr McDouall their most experienced packer. Replying to a query from Muriel Clayton, Sir Eric Maclagan wrote:

> McDouall estimates that there are some four lorry loads of stuff in the bomb-proof repository. I understand 'Woodwork' will also have some six or eight loads of furniture to go down, making ten or twelve loads in all – about a fortnight's work.

On top of this, twenty-eight lorry loads had been despatched from Kensington to Montacute at the outbreak of war, and it was expected that of that twenty lorry loads would be transferred to Westwood, a transfer that would take a further three or four weeks to complete.

This view shows, among an assortment of furniture and packing cases, one of the many thermo-hygrographs used in the quarry to monitor atmospheric conditions.

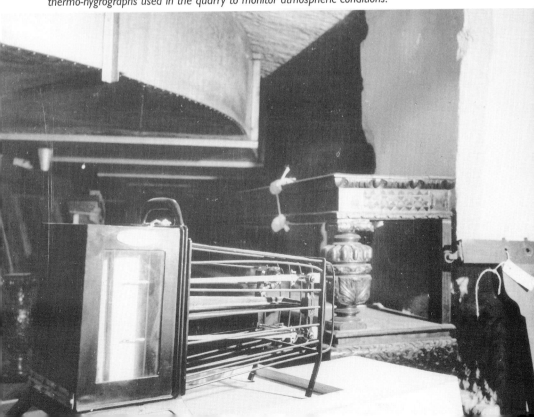

Part of the V&A collection of Terracottas stored in the quarry.

As information regarding the Westwood store filtered through the upper ranks of the museums and galleries community, Sir Eric Maclagan received a constant stream of requests from other national and provincial museums, as well as private collectors, seeking a safe haven for their treasures. In November 1941 a letter was received from Mr Mackintosh of the Science Museum asking:

Could you possibly be very kind and give me a small corner of your stone quarry, if you could spare it? It is to house the Wright Aeroplane (Kittyhawk) in absolute security.

Mackintosh went on to explain that Kittyhawk was on special loan to the museum from Orville Wright, and that:

By special request of the individual who is our liaison with Wright, it has not been sent to a country house and is still in our basement which I consider far from safe.

The aeroplane was packed in three cases, the largest of which contained the wings and measured seventeen feet by six feet, rather too large to fit through the repository doors. The problem was eventually overcome by dismantling the case and reassembling it once taken inside in pieces, and Kittyhawk spent the rest of the war in safety far below ground rather than in its natural environment above.

Meanwhile deliveries of British Museum artefacts from Boughton, Skipton Castle and Aberystwyth continued to arrive daily, the last four crates, containing thirteenth century glass from Salisbury Cathedral and from the parish church of Wilton that had been put into the care of the British Museum, arriving on 4 July 1942. Three weeks later 131 boxes of books and manuscripts arrived from the Bodleian Library, followed later the same day by many of the pictures from the National Portrait Gallery which had been in store since the outbreak of war at Mentmore House. A month earlier, on 16 June, officers at Westwood accepted the last of four lorry loads of paintings from the Kenwood collection. Cases containing these paintings were the last to be hauled into the quarry using narrow gauge locomotives belonging to the construction contractors. Two days later the locomotives were transferred to Spring Quarry in Corsham and thereafter laden railway trucks had to be manhandled into the repository.

As the quarry filled with treasures of inestimable value, some thought was given to local security which until now had been rather overlooked. British Museum warders previously employed at Bloomsbury were spread thinly over the whole range of emergency country house repositories and were able to carry out their daytime duty much as before, though obviously with less efficiency. Night-time security at Westwood, however, was notorious in the early days. The museums, via the agency of the Ministry of Works and Buildings, had contracted with the Wiltshire Constabulary to provide the services of one policeman from Bradford-on-Avon, the nearest town of any note, to patrol Westwood during the hours of darkness. Due to a severe manpower shortage in the Wiltshire police service this left Bradford-on-Avon and many of the surrounding parishes with no protection at all and in August 1942 the Constabulary gave notice that it was compelled to withdraw its officer from Westwood. It was then realized that the adjoining Royal Enfield factory, which shared a common entrance tunnel with the museum, was patrolled at night by a semi-private force of officers financed by the Ministry of Supply and known as the MoS Security Police. Eight officers and one sergeant patrolled the factory and there was always at least one officer on guard in the entrance tunnel. Negotiations were quickly entered into with Major Batten, an MI5 officer based at Corsham who was in overall charge of MoS security. The negotiations were successful and from 1 September the Ministry of Supply Security Police took over responsibility for night guard duty at the Westwood repository.

With Westwood available, Boughton House and Drayton were given up immediately, but those that were thought the best of the country houses were not deserted completely. The area around Skipton Castle was found to be remarkably free from the attention of enemy aircraft, and once the floors of the Banqueting Hall and the Toddy Room were suitably underpinned they were able to remain in use by the British Museum throughout the war. Space vacated at Aberystwyth after the best of the prints and manuscripts there were transferred to Westwood was soon filled with more books from the British Library evacuated from Bloomsbury, while another 65,000 volumes were transferred to the relative safety of the new Bodleian Building in Oxford. Tens of thousands of books remained in Bloomsbury, many of which perished on the night of 10 May 1941 when parts of the British Museum including the Roman British Room and the south-west Quadrant Bookstack were destroyed by incendiary bombs.

Although it initially appeared that now the fabric of the quarry was adequately dried the air-conditioning plant could maintain satisfactory conditions, by mid-April these conditions were deteriorating rapidly. During the first week of April humidity levels within the repository began to rise quickly, particularly in the British Museum's side of the quarry. This was not entirely unexpected as psychrometric tests conducted some years earlier in the War Office quarries at Corsham showed that from late spring until the end of October rising external temperatures, and therefore higher absolute moisture content in the air, inevitably resulted in very high humidity levels underground due to the more or less stable temperature there. Poor stacking had exacerbated the problem; many of the British Museum artefacts were in large packing cases that in places partially blocked the outlets from the ventilation system. Once these items were rearranged and stacked on wooden pallets to allow free circulation underneath the cases, conditions improved slightly.

On the morning of 18 April, however, conditions underground deteriorated with great rapidity, humidity rose to 95% within minutes and condensation appeared on the walls and packaging. It was obvious that there had been a major malfunction of the air-conditioning system but all the electrical recording instruments indicated that the plant was

A small part of the British Museum ethnographic collection stored in packing cases in the quarry. Note the use of woodden dunnage on the floor to allow air to circulate..

This photograph shows the atmospheric monitoring equipment in the Westwood plant room. The left-hand instrument is a ten-point temperature gauge with the main circulating fan control panel adjacent. The central instrument is a Cambridge chart recorder that maintains a permanent record of temperature and humidity within the repository. The equipment on the right-hand side consists of a series of control boxes for the 'Radiovisor' seven-point smoke detector and a Gent fire-alarm panel.

Power supply to the Westwood quarry complex was a complicated affair. Two independent 11Kv supplies fed one surface and two underground high-tension sub-stations. The east and west underground stations largely duplicated each other. This photo shows the west sub-station with switchgear marked up for Museum Lights, Museum Power and Enfield Factory Power.

operating normally and conditions were good. Then it was realized that the main plant and the recorders both worked off the same electricity supply so when power to the dehumidifiers failed, the recorders and the alarm systems also stopped.

A standby generating set, which would have obviated the disaster, was planned from the start of the project but in 1941 such equipment was impossible to obtain new and competition for second-hand plant was intense. A portable 18 Kw semi-diesel set was borrowed from the Bristol Aeroplane Company on a temporary basis and the firm of J. Gerber & Co were instructed by the MOWB to locate a more powerful alternator for permanent installation. The search for a suitable plant was protracted, but on 15 September Gerber & Co arranged the purchase of a very old 74 Kw Lister-Petter set from the Exe Valley Electricity Company of Dulverton for the enormous price of £860.

When delivered to Westwood it was found to be little better than scrap. While the 1931 Holland alternator was serviceable, the twenty-year-old two-cylinder, two-stroke diesel engine that drove it was not. There was no switchboard, starting, cooling or voltage regulating gear and the engine did not run. A thorough inspection revealed that all the main bearings and pistons needed replacing, but when the engineers contacted Petters of Loughborough for spares for the engine which, they said, was 'being erected in connection with works of great National importance', Petters replied:

> *The engine as you are aware was originally manufactured by Messrs Vickers-Petters Ltd of Ipswich, and as the engine type has been out of production for a good many years we have run out of spare parts and instruction books.*

Petters undertook to manufacture the necessary parts but these had still not been delivered in June 1942 and the Ministry of Works was becoming desperate. The new pistons finally arrived in September and by the end of the month the engine was sufficiently complete to be coaxed into motion, but despite all endeavours by the engineers it refused to run for more than a few minutes. The cause of the problem was pinned down to a brickwork expansion chamber near the bottom of the engine's exhaust shaft which had been almost filled with broken bricks and other debris by Wimpey's men in their hurry to complete the building work. Once this was cleared it was possible to keep the engine running although the voltage produced by the alternator fluctuated wildly. After much trouble an automatic regulator was found and fitted, and on 12 December preparations were made for the first full test run of the completed plant. The engine was still difficult to start and after five minutes running on-load unusual noises were heard coming from the cylinder head, followed by an enormous explosion that blew out the side wall of the exhaust silencer, wrecking electrical switchgear in the plant room under a shower of bricks and concrete and causing

The original Lister-Petter diesel generator which blew up shortly after this photograph was taken.

The failure of the original Petter generator in 1942 left the repository without an adequate back-up supply throughout the war years. This problem was not rectified until the late 1950s when a new alternator powered by a four-cylinder Crossley diesel engine was installed to upgrade the facility for its new, cold-war role.

irreparable internal damage to the engine. The old Lister-Petter set was thereupon abandoned and for the rest of the war the museums relied upon a range of borrowed or hired generators for standby purposes, the British Museum minute book for January 1943 recording that:

> Currently the standby electricity supply consists of a useless 60 Kw diesel and a fast-acting 18 Kw petrol generator. A further temporary unit was removed as it caused too many difficulties. Meanwhile a second 11 Kv grid supply is being installed from a new sub-station at Trowbridge and a hired generator installed on the surface until the problems with the main underground set can be rectified.

There were no changes made to this arrangement until the mid-1950s when a brand new Crossley-engined alternator set was installed as part of a refurbishment plan intended to prepare Westwood for a similar role in nuclear war, but that is another story.

For some time after the quarry was handed over to the museums there were still regular complaints that the air-conditioning plant was not working satisfactorily and that traces of mildew had appeared on some of the tapestries.

Concern aroused in a report by Sir Eric Maclagan reached the highest levels, and in February 1943, in a letter to Lord Portal the new Chief Commissioner of Works, R.A. Butler, the Minister of Education, stated:

> All the most valuable works of art of the museums, amounting to many millions, are at present housed in the quarry at Westwood, and as Minister responsible for their custody, I am alarmed by the conditions to which Maclagan draws attention. I have, of course, no expert knowledge of the measures that can be taken to secure an even temperature and to avoid humidity, but I feel sure you will agree that it is imperative that a thorough investigation of the apparatus installed for these purposes should be made without delay.

Independent tests conducted by the National Physical Laboratory concluded that the plant was adequate for its purpose and that the fault lay with its inefficient operation. To ensure future reliability and proper plant room discipline comprehensive operating instructions were drawn up which required the plant attendants to adhere to a set routine and maintain a minute-by-minute log of their actions in response to changing ambient conditions. Although these new procedures had an immediate beneficial effect, the rapid deterioration in conditions within the repository when the plant failed gave rise to other concerns. Sir Eric Maclagan drew attention to the vulnerability of the air-conditioning plant, which had cost £12,000 to install and which was very close to the bottom of an air inlet shaft that had little or no protection against bombs. Maclagan noted that:

> We are entirely dependant upon the engines, the humidity rises the second they stop. It shows what state the place would be in if the engine room were out of action.

Much of the surface land at Westwood remained semi-derelict for nearly forty years after the end of the war, but housing development is now slowly encroaching upon it. In 2001 an imposing detached house was built on the site of the museum air shaft seen opposite, but because the ventilation shaft is still in use by Wansdyke Security it had to be retained. The elegant little gazebo seen in this photograph, built to match the house, actually conceals the old shaft and a range of service ducts.

All the ventilation shaft tops at Westwood were provided with substantial red-brick buildings that gave some degree of blast protection and protection against the risk of penetration by a direct hit by enemy bombs. Their design also ensured the maximum separation between fresh air inlet and foul air outlet ducts. The building in this picture contains the main air ducts for the museum air-conditioning plant, the exhaust from the standby generator and an eighty-foot vertical ladder which acts as an emergency escape route from the underground powerhouse.

At such a late stage little could be done to improve the situation. It was impossible to move the plant room, but changes were made to the shaft head buildings to render them a little more bomb-proof and at the same time the opportunity was taken to incorporate improved filters and filter cleaning plant in the modified buildings.

With most of the technical difficulties ironed out the quarry settled into a reasonably uneventful routine until the end of the war. Museum staff continued with the routine tasks of cataloguing and conservation under the overall management of Mr Gadd, the British Museum's Keeper of Assyrian and Egyptian Antiquities. Later this responsibility was rotated among the various departmental heads of both the V&A and the British Museum.

Westwood had become the nation's great treasure-house and on 31 March 1943 a visit was arranged for HM Queen Mary who spent much of the war at nearby Badminton House, home of the Duke of Beaufort. Following the visit, Sidenham, the Queen's Private Secretary, wrote to Sir John Forsdyke that:

Queen Mary has commanded me to write and thank you very much indeed for her most enjoyable and successful visit to Westwood yesterday afternoon. Her Majesty has been very anxious to see how the National Treasures from the museums and galleries are stored in places of safety during the war, and it was therefore of the greatest interest to her to inspect the underground quarry at Westwood.

7

THE NATIONAL GALLERY AND MANOD QUARRY

Some five weeks before the Museums and Galleries Air Raid Precautions Committee first met in 1933 to discuss a unified approach to safeguarding the nation's cultural treasures in event of war, the National Gallery trustees had already agreed an independent strategy. Detailed planning for the evacuation was left in the hands of Francis Rawlins, the National Gallery's newly appointed scientific advisor who had just come down from Cambridge and was in the process of establishing the gallery's Scientific Section. He was the first to recognize the pressing need for stable storage conditions and conducted numerous experiments in this field at the temporary country house repositories and later at the underground repository at Manod quarry. An ardent railway enthusiast since early youth, his encyclopaedic knowledge of the British railway timetable was put to good use during the evacuation to North Wales. Several buildings in North Wales and Gloucestershire were initially selected as emergency repositories but by 1939 this list had been whittled down to just four:

- Old Quarries at Avening in Gloucestershire
- Prichard Jones Hall at the University of Wales in Bangor
- Penrhyn Castle
- National Library of Wales at Aberystwyth

The Welsh repositories were all solidly constructed large buildings, all too easily identifiable by aerial surveillance and prominent targets for enemy bombing, but chosen because in 1939 it was thought that the north-west coast of Wales would be beyond the range of enemy bombers.

As a result of the intensive works programme under way at Trafalgar Square during 1938/9, including construction of the 'armoured corridor', the installation of new lifts to enable pictures to be brought down from the upper floor galleries quickly, and the provision of new concrete access-ways and loading docks to the rear of the building, it had not been possible to make simultaneous, detailed preparations at the country houses. However, some screens and other stores likely to be useful when the time came to occupy the repositories were accumulated and plans were made to recruit local members of the British Legion to supplement the gallery's own staff for guard duty.

It had been agreed in 1938 that all transport would be by rail and that for all but a few of the pictures (whose dimension on their shortest axis exceeded seven feet) standard door-to-door railway containers of the type that could be unloaded from the railway trucks directly onto motor

lorries would be used. About a dozen of the gallery's pictures were too large for the railway containers and for these special transit cases were manufactured by the Ministry of Works. Arrangements were made with the railway companies for two double-bogie low-loader railway wagons of the type sometimes used to transport heavy machinery like transformers or ship's engines to be adapted for the transhipment of the large pictures. The suspensions of these wagons were adjusted to give a soft ride and they were fitted with continuous brakes, unusual at that time on freight vehicles, to allow high-speed running.

Loaded aboard the special well-wagons, all but one of the large packing cases came within the standard railway loading gauge. The exception contained the van Dyck 'Charles I on Horseback' which stood thirteen feet six inches high and extreme measures were required to bring it within gauge. The case was constructed in the form of a right-angle triangle with fixings attached to hold the painting in a position parallel with the hypotenuse. Even then it could not be brought within railway clearance unless loaded eccentrically on the well-wagon. A loading diagram was then prepared and the case secured to the wagon with heavy timber baulks.

On 23 August 1939, in view of the critical political situation, Sir Kenneth Clark sought permission from the Treasury to close one exhibition room at the National Gallery in order to begin packing the contents in preparation for evacuation. On the following day, Thursday 24th, the whole gallery was closed to the public and the evacuation began, the first two containers with 222 pictures being dispatched to Old Quarries at Avening that day. By midnight on Saturday 2 September all the paintings of any importance were gone. On Monday morning Sir Kenneth Clark was able to inform the Treasury that:

Old Quarries at Avening, home of Lord Lee of Fareham. The single-storey building to the right of the main house is Lord Lee's private gallery which was built in 1938.

An interior view of Lord Lee's gallery at Old Quarries.

The evacuation of all the pictures from the Gallery is now complete. All pictures of any value had been removed before the weekend. Yesterday and today we have sent off the first two containers of books from the library as well as two containers with some mediocre pictures which seemed just worth saving. I have decided to leave about twenty-five pictures which cannot under any circumstances be considered of interest or value. Most of them are copies, some of considerable surprise.

I have had reports from Maclaren at Aberystwyth and Davies at Bangor. The former have been most satisfactory, the only damage reported being occasional rubbing of varnish. Davies' report contains one or two cases of scratches but only in unimportant places.

Sir Kenneth went himself to inspect the 222 paintings sent to Lord Lee's house, Old Quarries, at Avening and reported:

I inspected them very carefully and could not find the least trace of damage. They are hung up and Lord Lee has made the most thorough arrangements for their safe keeping. From the point of view of temperature, security and invigilation his gallery is excellent.

Lord Lee of Fareham was Deputy Chairman of the Fine Arts Commission, a Trustee of the National Gallery and the Wallace Collection and Deputy Chairman of the Management Committee of the Courtauld Institute, Governor of Cheltenham College and editor of the 'English Heritage' series. In 1921 he gave the Chequers estate to the nation. At Old Quarries he maintained an extensive private collection with a dedicated staff who, during the war, also undertook all warding

83

Immediately after the end of the war, Old Quarries became a boy's school and has subsequently remained in institutional use. Alterations to the gallery building, including the addition of a second floor below a new mansard roof, were made by the Home Farm Trust, the current owners, who use the house and its grounds as a home for people with learning difficulties.

and maintenance duties with regard to the National Gallery pictures stored there.

SCHEDULE OF DEPARTURE

Aug 24	Avening	2 containers	222 paintings
Aug 25	Bangor	4 containers	195 paintings including 10 on loan and 30 from the Gilbenkian collection
Aug 26	Bangor	5 special cases	15 large paintings
Aug 27	Aberystwyth	2 containers	187 paintings
Aug 28	Bangor	2 containers	128 paintings
Aug 29	Bangor	2 containers	145 paintings
Aug 30	Aberystwyth	2 containers	60 paintings
Sept 1	Aberystwyth	2 containers	227 paintings consisting of 99 National Gallery oils, 64 loaned oils, 26 loaned watercolours, 6 parcels of drawings and one of engravings.
Sept 2	Bangor	2 containers	218 paintings
Sept 3	Aberystwyth	2 containers	47 paintings and 100 boxes of library material
Sept 4	Aberystwyth	1 container	41 boxes of library material
Sept 5	Aberystwyth	2 containers	99 boxes of library material
Sept 6	Aberystwyth	1 container	Photographic collection

The movement and distribution of so much property of such immense monetary value raised questions about security. At first the concerns were just about the security of the art treasures whilst in transit, but later questions were raised about the general safety of the country house repositories, where physical security was inevitably more difficult to achieve than in the purpose-built London galleries. Towards the end of August 1939 Bennitt at the Office of Works asked Mr R.S. Wells of the Home Office whether, regarding police protection of art treasures in transit and at the country repositories, he could 'arrange for a certain amount of Police protection, especially in view of IRA activities at night.'

This request provoked a heated debate about how far police responsibility extended in this case and whether or not such police officers as might be detailed to the task should or should not be armed. The Metropolitan Police Commissioner agreed that he was responsible for artefacts in transit while in London and that:

> One Police Constable, who is to be armed with a service revolver, will accompany each vehicle, remaining with it until relieved by a Railway Policeman or other competent railway authority at the railway station.

He was not, however, in favour of allowing police officers or guards patrolling the country houses to be armed, arguing that such houses were not officially defined as 'Vulnerable Places' and that criminal interference would not 'impede the conduct of the war'. The Commissioner went on later to express his opinion that:

> The criminal classes who might wish to steal property from these places have anyhow been conscripted into the service.

Opinions among members of the Museums and Galleries ARP Committee were divided on the subject. John Beresford, the committee chairman wrote to the Home Office informing them that:

> Sir John Forsdyke was particularly emphatic that it would not be desirable for the wardens to carry shotguns; it would be unwise from the standpoint of calling attention to the places concerned for them to be marching about with guns.

Sir John did concede that it might be advisable for the warders to carry revolvers when inside the buildings.

UNIVERSITY OF BANGOR – PRICHARD JONES HALL

At the University of Wales in Bangor, the National Gallery occupied the sealed inner hall of the Prichard Jones Hall. At first security was delegated to nine locally recruited members of the British Legion but by the end of September local concern about the loyalty of some of these men led to their replacement by police reservists.

Only a few pictures were stored at Bangor even though the storage conditions there were better than at many of the other emergency repositories. The most pressing problem at Bangor was the university's heating system. Although the plant, which consisted of several antiquated coke-fired boilers, was inherently difficult to manage, this was not the major difficulty but was exacerbated by the long-standing resident engineer-cum-boilerman who had a reputation as an obstinate and difficult man. It was impossible to recruit new staff and consequently the working of the system was extremely erratic, causing wide fluctuations in temperature, particularly during periods of changeable weather. Treasury funding was sought to replace the existing steam heating by electric heaters due to their greater controllability and also because it would enable the National Gallery to dispense with the university engineer, but this was not forthcoming and the plan was abandoned in October 1939.

NATIONAL LIBRARY OF WALES AT ABERYSTWYTH

In Aberystwyth the National Gallery occupied rooms on the top floor of the National Gallery of Wales where several hundred pictures were stored. Conditions inside the building, parts of which were only recently completed, were excellent, having been purpose-built for the storage of delicate materials. The greatest problem at Aberystwyth was the risk of fire and aerial bombardment with so many valuable pictures concentrated in a small area.

PENRHYN CASTLE

The accommodation offered by Lord Penrhyn at Penrhyn Castle consisted of the Old Dining Hall which was the largest room in the house, chosen because the high doorways allowed the passage of all but the largest pictures, and two garages, formerly coach-houses, the largest of which had doors eleven feet three inches high, tall enough to admit even van Dyck's 'Charles 1 on Horseback' on its side. The smaller garage was less suitable and consisted of just half of a larger building which was to be partitioned with asbestos sheeting at the gallery's expense. The other half would continue to house Lord Penrhyn's cars. Storage space was offered free of charge for an indefinite period but it was agreed that the Office of Works would install separately metered electric heating in the rooms occupied by the National Gallery. Heavy, curtained shutters over the Dining Room windows prevented too great a drop in night-time temperature.

Stabilization of conditions in the garages was a more difficult task. The garages' thin walls, their ill-fitting doors that let in draughts, rain and rats, and a highly exposed position allowed wide fluctuations in temperature and humidity that simply mirrored external weather conditions. Measures adopted to alleviate this situation ran counter to accepted practice in that all the openings and gaps were stopped-up as securely as possible with old rags to reduce the ingress of external air

Lord Penrhyn's monstrous Victorian gothic pile, Penrhyn Castle, the troubled home of the majority of the National Gallery's pictures from 1939 until 1941.

and electric tubular heaters installed to maintain a reasonable temperature. Electric fans ran constantly to prevent air stagnation but the doors were opened only very occasionally to allow the intake of fresh air. Surprisingly this technique was entirely successful, a reasonable relative humidity was maintained at 70°C, no mildew was formed and there were no significant signs of contraction stresses in the canvases or frames.

FEARS FOR THE SAFETY OF THE COLLECTION

By the late spring of 1940 the future of the north Wales repositories was already becoming uncertain. Access to airfields in northern France allowed the Luftwaffe to range freely over most of Britain, effectively negating most of the advantages of the country house dispersal scheme. But there were other more local problems too. In February the University of Wales student magazine *Omnibus* carried an article about the National Gallery pictures stored in the Prichard Jones Hall and the University Registrar feared that the gallery might take steps to invoke the Defence of the Realm Act to prevent further disclosures. Gibson at the National Gallery headquarters replied that he did not think that the article would do much harm but stated that he would support the Registrar in any action he thought fit.

By 24 May, however, Martin Davies, the National Gallery man at Bangor was sufficiently agitated to write to Gibson that:

Rawlins and I are feeling considerably agitated about the safety of the pictures here in the immediate future, not so much on account of danger from bombing as from civil disturbance on a large scale. According to Rawlins' evidence (from our former embassy in Berlin and from Rome) organized riots must accompany any attempt at invasion, and, as you agreed in your last letter, Prichard Jones Hall and Penrhyn cannot be effectively defended against a mob.

It would seem that the chances of preservation would be increased by distribution of a few very important pictures. The houses already reserved for this purpose in North Wales would be too difficult to control and housing the pictures there might increase the general risk. Before bringing up to you again, for your very serious consideration, a proposal for distribution, we thought it fit to enquire about storage space within ten miles of here suitable for fifteen or twenty moderate sized pictures of great value.

As your decision on policy seems to us urgent we wish to tell you that we have inspected at Caernarvon Castle storage space of A1 quality in the basement of one of the towers. The building is controlled by the Office of Works and is easy of access from Bangor (nine miles by train, bus or car). We should like at once to set in hand the adaptation for heating all of this room (which should be easy) and prepare a list of men for guard duty. We should like to make this room ready to receive pictures at the shortest notice; the railways have given Rawlins a most explicit guarantee of immediate transport in the case of civil disturbance.

Although even one extra storage place for the pictures that matter would, we think, be of value, their number is I suppose about 100, and a further one or two places would provide a more reasonable distribution of risk. One house near Caernarvon has been recommended to us; we have not seen it but the owner is said to be trustworthy. I do not think that two other suitable houses in the region need be impossible to find.

*The pros and cons of distribution are too complicated for discussion in a letter. Rawlins and I have agreed about it and as you see are both pro as things have now become, but the decision on such a matter is not ours. We are however, convinced that if distribution is approved **immediate** preparations are necessary in order that it may take place as soon as the time comes. If therefore you do approve will you obtain sanction from the Treasury for extra guards? Meanwhile I am striving to increase the precautions at Prichard Jones Hall and Penrhyn but there is nothing very useful to be done and the responsibility for so much collected together is a trifle wearing.*

A few days later, on 27 May, Francis Rawlins, writing with similar agitation to the Office of Works from his temporary headquarters at the University of Bangor recorded that:

Davies and I are becoming increasingly apprehensive about the high concentration of valuable pictures here and at Penrhyn. Our concern is not particularly with the possibility of bombs but with the possibility of activities by the 5th Column. You will recall that I mentioned to you in a conversation my own gleanings of local information about this.

This feeling of apprehension was shared by the RAF which had recently commissioned an enormous underground bomb store at Llanberis that was to become a key element in its logistics organization. The bomb store, according to the depot's Operations Record Book, was

mainly staffed by civilian labourers under a small contingent of RAF Officers. There is a shortage of civilian staff, who are all local, Welsh, and very nationalistic – more interested in Home Rule than work. Likewise the Security Wardens are Welsh and are not considered trustworthy.

LORD PENRHYN BECOMES DIFFICULT

After only a few weeks at Penrhyn Castle staff of the National Gallery realized that the house had not been a good choice. The fact that its relative remoteness no longer offered any security against bombardment was only one item in a catalogue of shortcomings. Much of the difficulty was rooted in an intense clash of personalities between Lord Penrhyn and Sir Martin Davies, who was Assistant Keeper at the National Gallery and in personal charge of the pictures at the Castle. Davies' personal correspondence makes it quite clear that he found Penrhyn's attitude obnoxious and constantly obstructive. On 5 June Davies reported some of his problems to his superiors in London, noting, in great exasperation:

For your most secret ear: One of our troubles at Penrhyn Castle is that the owner is celebrating the war by being fairly constantly drunk. He stumbled with a dog into the Dining Room a few days ago: this will not happen again. Yesterday he smashed up his car, and, I believe, himself a little, so perhaps the problem has solved itself for the moment.

Just a few days later Davies informed the Office of Works that as a consequence of the British Army's retreat from Dunkirk:

> *A peculiar situation has arisen at Penrhyn Castle. A thousand troops back from Flanders are being sent to Bangor to rest. Lord Penrhyn, without consulting me, has agreed to receive them at the Castle. For sentimental reasons I do not feel inclined to veto the billeting of the troops, though I maintained to Lord Penrhyn's agent, with whom I transact all business, that I could have done so.*

Whilst sympathizing with Davies' problem and recognizing the potential security implications, Bennitt was compelled to reply:

> *I am afraid the National Gallery would not be thought well of if they tried to turn out the British Expeditionary Force.*

Within days Bennitt was confronted with more bad news from Penrhyn when William Gibson from the National Gallery informed him about Lord Penrhyn's latest scheme to compromise the gallery's security at the Castle. Gibson wrote:

> *I have just heard from Davies that Lord Penrhyn now proposes to let his castle to a girls' school, keeping a small corner for himself and leaving the National Gallery pictures where they are. I can see that if he is feeling short of money we cannot prevent him economizing in this way and a girls' school would at least be less dangerous than soldiers. But the entry of a large number of unknown people certainly increases our risk. If you could write to Lord Penrhyn pointing out that we have preserved him from the use of other government departments, evacuees, etc, it may have some effect.*

An intervention from the Office of Works had little effect, but the girls' school scheme came to naught. It was generally assumed that neither Penrhyn nor his agents had been involved in negotiation with any such school nor had they any specific institution in mind, but that the intention was simply to coerce the Office of Works to agree to a commercial rent for the Castle. As a precaution against any similar such ruse, the gallery and the Office of Works investigated several alternative properties in the immediate vicinity which might be occupied at short notice. Among the most promising were Coed Coch near Abergele and Rhug at Corwen. Others that were rejected included Qwrych Castle, a huge empty building of little use because it was too damp and had only tiny doorways, and Sir William Watkin Wynn's house, Wynnstay near Ruabon, which was rejected on account of its proximity to a TNT factory.

Unable to make financial headway by more insidious means, Lord Penrhyn, through his factotum, made an outright demand for an economic, retrospective rent from the National Gallery in September

1940. In utter frustration, Davies wrote to the Office of Works:

You will see that one after another of our Country House owners are thinking of ways of making money out of us. They seem to forget that we have saved them the great inconvenience of compulsory evacuees planted on them. Their willingness to make sacrifice in war does not seem to be great, and one cannot help suspecting that of such are the followers of Pétain made.

Later in the same letter, Davies continued:

Lord Penrhyn was recently approached by the Board of Education with a view to the house being taken over either for its own headquarters purposes or for the Royal College of Art, but owing to his obstructive attitude the proposal fell through completely.

By our occupation of a very small portion of the house we have kept the whole of the rest free from evacuees and military occupation. We have always regarded this as something of a quid-pro-quo for the so-called 'generosity' of the owner in letting us use a portion of the house which anyhow is almost useless to him.

In the vain hope of avoiding further unpleasantness with Lord Penrhyn, the Office of Works finally agreed in November upon an annual payment of £250 for the use of the house. Justifying his demands Penrhyn commented that: 'amongst other things, increased taxation and the cost of living has made it very difficult for large landowners to live in their houses.' This was to some extent true and was a portent of the gradual decline of the English landed estate initiated by the socialist policies of the post-war labour government. High taxation and shortages of staff, most of whom left the great houses in droves during the war and later showed no inclination to return under pre-war conditions, left many estates unviable in the harsh, post-war world.

Crosswood House, another of the Welsh houses occupied by the National Gallery, was leased to the government in 1946 in lieu of death duties and until recently was occupied by the Welsh Agricultural Advisory Service. Many others became hospitals or local government institutions, or like Penrhyn Castle and many similar properties were passed to the National Trust. Far too many other fine houses of lesser merit or in locations unsuitable for commercial development were simply destroyed by their owners. In Somerset, for example, the Mendip hills are littered with lost estates; great houses like Woodborough Lodge (which had a stay of execution while serving for a few years as the regional headquarters of the National Coal Board), Charlton House, and Ashwick Grove, now marked by no more than overgrown gateposts in a roadside hedge.

However, no matter what the justification, the payment to Lord Penrhyn set a precedent that the Office of Works had hoped to avoid. A couple of weeks later they were compelled to accede to a similar demand from the owner of Drayton House for a retrospective rent of £250, and others were to follow.

By the end of June 1940, the difficulties created by the threat of civil unrest and Lord Penrhyn's recalcitrant attitude were compounded by additional fears of attack from the German aircraft, en route to bomb Liverpool docks, which regularly passed directly above Bangor and Penrhyn. A serious risk at Penrhyn was that of fire as incendiary bombs could wreak havoc on the two-acre roof of the Castle, much of which was virtually inaccessible to the fire-watchers. In July the gallery's Director and Chairman, Mr Samuel Courtauld, examined the problem and decided that further evacuation involving greater fragmentation of the collection was inevitable, but that underground storage was the only truly secure option. Rawlins and Davies, however, were of the opinion that the immediate problem was of safeguarding the collection against the threat of civil insurrection, which they considered imminent. To effect a short-term solution Sir Kenneth Clark was asked to request funding for the acquisition of storage space for 110 of the very best pictures at three further properties within a twenty-mile radius of Bangor: Caernarvon Castle, which had already been inspected, Plas-y-Bryn at Bontnewydd, and Crosswood House, a few miles from Aberystwyth. At the Treasury, Mr Gatcliff, upon whose desk virtually all the controversial matters regarding underground projects landed, responded with some cynicism:

> Personally I very much wish that many of these treasures would stay scattered about, since we would all appreciate them much more if we had to go on a pilgrimage to see them and only saw one or two at a time, instead of getting artistic indigestion and headaches by wandering around the National Gallery.

With Treasury consent a small number of pictures were transferred to Caernarvon and Bontnewydd towards the end of the year, sealed in shadow boxes to protect them as much as possible from temperature fluctuations. Arrangements were then made to transfer the seventy very finest paintings to Crosswood House, but before this could be done some detailed preparations were required. These works took longer than anticipated to complete, but by mid-January 1941 it was anticipated that the house would be ready by the end of the month. By that time construction was in hand at the new underground repository at Manod and as yet there was no indication of the delays that subsequently developed. The planned dispersal to Crosswood was therefore questioned on the grounds that the disruption this would cause was unnecessary as it was expected that Manod, the final solution, would be ready in a few weeks. The fragile situation in all the existing repositories, and particularly the difficulties with Lord Penrhyn, made at least a partial evacuation unavoidable and on 11 February the first container of pictures was transferred to Crosswood.

The ballroom elevation of Crosswood House. A temporary porch was added to the French window to the right of the curved central bay to accommodate National Gallery warders.

Eight miles from Aberystwyth, Crosswood House, home of the Earl of Lisburne, was geographically well placed for use as an emergency dispersal from Penrhyn Castle, but in most other respects it was a disaster. Lisburne initially agreed quite readily to the National Gallery using the Library (sometimes referred to as the Large Dining Room) at Crosswood free of charge, but thereafter made life for the gallery staff there as difficult as it had been at Penrhyn. His lordship refused to have National Gallery staff or security personnel at large in his house, insisting that a temporary external porch attached to the Library's French windows should be erected and that staff should be confined there.

There were similar difficulties over the heating of the Library. Crosswood was heated by an antiquated and highly temperamental coal-fired boiler in the cellar which circulated hot water around the house in large diameter pipes to a range of cast-iron radiators. The system was virtually uncontrollable once the furnace was lit, so in winter the house was intolerably hot or bitterly cold. It was impossible to isolate individual rooms for heating purposes, so when it was necessary to heat the Library to ensure adequate conditions for the pictures stored there, the rest of the house was heated also. Because the boiler could not be regulated the temperature in the Library sometimes rose to dangerously high levels and the air became so dry that it crackled. Gallery staff were faced with the unique problem of having to increase the humidity in one of their repositories, a task achieved by covering the heating pipes and radiators in the library with old blankets saturated in water from a nearby stream.

Shortly after the National Gallery arrived at Crosswood Lord Lisburne discovered that he, like the owners of other country houses selected to protect the national treasures, was likely to foot the bill for heating expenses. Lisburne immediately ruled that the central heating system was not to be fired-up, his justification being that in his straitened circumstances due to recent increases in taxation to pay for the war he could no longer afford the ten tons of anthracite it consumed each week. Informing them of his decision, Lisburne told the Ministry of Works that:

> *I have seen the plumber who knows my house and has looked after the heating system for years, and he tells me that a separate boiler would be the only satisfactory way, and that it would be possible for you to put a small independent boiler in my present boiler-room and connect it up to the library, and put in your own radiators as required. The present radiators could be shut off. Of course, I must make it clear that no walls in the library can be touched. These are hand painted and of great value.*

The Earl's engineer confirmed that 'a system of valves and cocks could be introduced, enabling this to be done' and thereby reduce anthracite consumption to about four tons per week. A.K. Davies was not impressed with this plan and wrote to his trustees that while discussing the Earl's proposals with men from the Ministry of Works he had been told that:

> *Lord Lisburne was not keen on having the National Gallery on his premises and that certain difficulties had been experienced owing to the Department requiring alterations to the central heating system.*

Davies suggested instead that electric heating be installed, utilizing Crosswood's small, 100-volt private generating plant. The MOWB engineers calculated that a minimum of seven Kilowatts, or a current of seventy amps, would be needed adequately to heat the library and that this was far beyond the plant capacity. So, much against the wishes of Lord Lisburne, the decrepit old central heating system continued to burn up ten tons of anthracite each week for the benefit of the National Gallery, but the Earl had other revenue-raising schemes in mind that he hoped would more than compensate.

On 25 September 1940 Lisburne informed the National Gallery that 'in order to raise a little money to pay the additional war time tax burden' he intended to let the house to a girls' school, giving the gallery the options of paying an economic rent for the whole house or sharing its facilities with the schoolgirls. The latter, he knew, would be quite unacceptable to the National Gallery on the grounds of security. After five months of rather unpleasant negotiation the National Gallery agreed to pay £80 per annum as a contribution towards the heating costs at Crosswood House, this being a sum sufficient to dissuade the Earl of Lisburne from pursuing the girls' school option.

Unaware of the impending delays in completion of the underground repository at Manod, gallery staff at Crosswood thought by February 1941 that the pictures there would be moved out at any day, and were less inclined to tolerate Lord Lisburne's peculiarities. Lisburne, for his part, realized somewhat belatedly that the presence of the National Gallery was infinitely preferable to that of refugee children from

Liverpool or Birmingham. The pictures were eventually transferred to Manod on 14 August, and shortly afterwards Lord Lisburne wrote to Sir Kenneth Clark offering his house for whatever purpose he might see fit. Sir Kenneth replied:

> *Now that the pictures are gone we have no immediate use for the space, but a scheme has recently been made for many private and some public collections of art treasures to move to safer places in the country, and also for helping the provincial museums who have not already moved their best things.*

Early the following year Birmingham Museum and Art Gallery agreed a scheme to disperse its collection amongst a number of country houses beyond the midlands industrial area. Ceramics from the collection were housed in the library at Crosswood where they were later joined by similar artefacts from the Royal collection. Elsewhere, Birmingham Museum occupied the billiard room at Fox Hill in Broadway, the drawing room at Stanage Park near Knighton, ten rooms at Elford Park in Tamworth, parts of Packwood House in Hockley Heath, and Henley Hall in Shropshire.

Meanwhile Samuel Courtauld, who had the ear of the Prime Minister, pressed his ideas upon Churchill, questioning even whether the pictures should be sent out of the country, probably to Canada, or be buried deep underground, to which Churchill replied: 'If possible they should be put in caves.'

The task of locating suitable underground storage fell upon the shoulders of the gallery's scientific advisor, Francis Rawlins. Numerous caves, disused quarries and natural defiles that could be roofed over were investigated and dismissed as useless for one reason or another. The search seemed futile until, on 17 September 1940, Rawlins, in company with Mr Halcrow of the civil engineering firm William Halcrow & Partners, discovered Manod Quarry and declared it eminently suitable.

The following day Rawlins and Halcrow met the quarry owners' representatives to discuss terms and were told, somewhat disingenuously, that an option on the quarry could only be held open for two days because several other government departments were also interested. On the 19th Rawlins sped back to London to discuss the matter with Samuel Courtauld; a meeting with Treasury officials was hastily arranged for the following day and at 12.00 noon on the 20th an outline plan presented. By 1.00 pm an agreement had been reached and Francis Rawlins arranged for Mr Mole, Senior Architect at the Ministry of Works, to contact the Ministry's North Wales Division to inspect the quarry that day. Brigadier H. Temple Richards, Senior Civil Engineer of the Ministry of Works Defence Architects Department, was delegated to take charge of the project should the inspector's report prove favourable.

Meanwhile, the Treasury had no intention of allowing the Manod Quarrying Company to dictate terms. From the Office of Works, Bennitt informed Francis Rawlins that:

> *The Treasury Solicitor has advised that they can requisition, and they have bluffed the owners into keeping the place for them.*

Three weeks later Mr Bennitt for the Office of Works made formal application to the Treasury to acquire the quarry:

> *I am directed by the First Commissioner of His Majesty's Office of Works to state for the information of the Lords Commissioners of His Majesty's Treasury that it is proposed at the instance of the Trustees of the National Gallery to adapt for the storage of pictures evacuated from the Gallery certain unused slate quarries the property of the Manod Slate Quarry Ltd, Blaenau Ffestiniog.*

The acquisition of underground storage for the National Gallery ran contrary to current government policy regarding the general provision of underground accommodation and also caused some disquiet regarding the low priority given to public deep-level air-raid shelters. The National Gallery was particularly concerned about the repercussions upon its public image should it become known that funds had been made available to shelter its elitist trifles while the population of London had been categorically denied the same protection. This was a particularly sensitive time for the Museums and Galleries ARP Committee for there was already a row developing with the Home Office about the British Museum presence in the Aldwych Tube. Space there was occupied that could, some said, be better used as a public air-raid shelter. This matter was discussed by the Office of Works and the Cabinet Office, who concluded that:

> *There seems to be no risk of the scheme reacting on shelter policy generally because no one who is lucky enough to get to North Wales will be content to remain unsheltered there, and these caves, being approached through a 250-yard tunnel, are not a particularly attractive place.*

The setting of Manod Quarry is perhaps as breathtaking a location as could be found anywhere in the British Isles. At the end of a five-mile private track in the Snowdon mountains, high above the rain-lashed, bleak slate village of Blaenau Ffestiniog with its rows of slate-block cottages capped by grey slate roofs, hidden in the shadows of the grey slate mountains, nowhere could be more forbidding or remote. Slate quarrying had continued at Manod for many decades and the mountain was a honeycomb of huge chambers often over 100 feet in height. Slate was quarried in three dimensions, so the worked-out chambers extended not just laterally into the mountain but were worked one above the other in levels, sometimes with floors little more than three feet thick separating them. In places these floors have collapsed, leaving vast open spaces several hundred feet high. Interspersed amongst the great chambers and working faces were smaller diameter tunnels or adits sometimes several miles in length, blasted out to drain away the seepage water that would otherwise accumulate and drown the workings.

Some areas of the quarry were still being worked but five worked-out chambers were identified that could be sealed off from the rest. The whole of level 'A' of the quarry (the most recently worked-out area) was acquired by the Ministry of Works together with level 'B' immediately below, which was taken in order to quarantine the area and ensure physical security.

Plans were prepared for the erection of six air-conditioned storage buildings inside the quarry caverns and it was hoped that much of the construction contract could be given to the slate company as limited compensation for their having been unable to auction the site to the highest bidder. The Office of Works explained to the Treasury that:

> *Clearing works and roads can most readily be carried out by the quarry owners who have plant and materials ready on the spot. It is proposed to make arrangements for the work to be done by them on the basis of actual cost plus a fixed fee to be negotiated. The residual value to the quarry owner of any works will be taken into account.*

The rest of the building and fitting-out was to be offered to local tradesmen by competitive tender. Ultimately an acceptable 'costs-plus-profit' contract could not be agreed with the Manod Quarrying Company and the work was finally awarded to Sir William Mowlem for a fixed fee of £5,070. Later in the war 'costs-plus-profit' contracts were widely used, particularly for the construction of airfields and ordnance factories. The system was much abused, being regarded by many contractors as a licence to print money and offered many opportunities for fraud.

A schedule of work was prepared towards the end of September and it was hoped that the gallery would have occupation of the quarry by Christmas 1940. Major building works included:

- New road near quarry entrance £1000
- Repairs to existing road £500
- Power and air lines £1000
- Improvement to entrance tunnel £875
- Sheeting wet roof £100
- Walling-off disused workings £200
- Clearing debris £900
- Building 50,000 feet of brick wall for storage buildings . . . £4000
- Wallboards and ceilings £500
- Hydroscopic curtain £2000
- New studio near entrance £1000
- Alterations to existing external offices £100
- Heating and lighting £4000

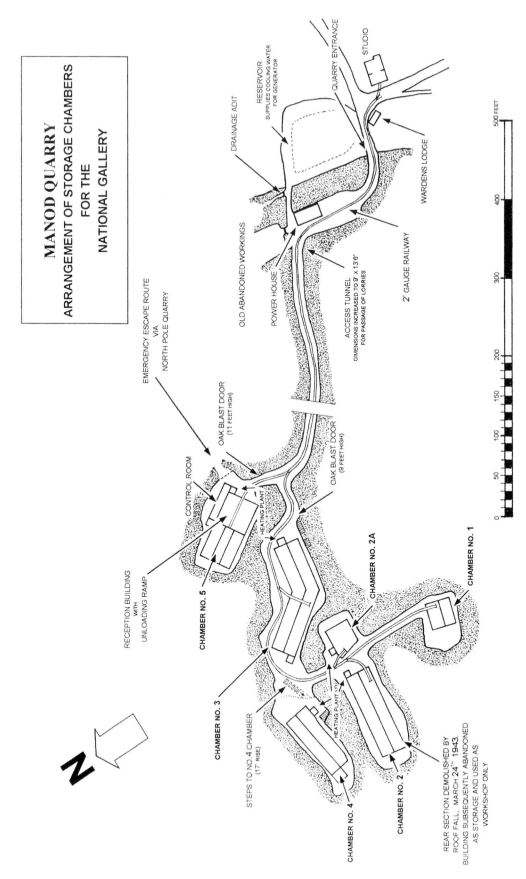

MANOD QUARRY
ARRANGEMENT OF STORAGE CHAMBERS
FOR THE
NATIONAL GALLERY

N

STUDIO

QUARRY ENTRANCE

RESERVOIR
SUPPLIES COOLING WATER
FOR GENERATOR

DRAINAGE ADIT

WARDENS LODGE

2' GAUGE RAILWAY

OLD ABANDONED WORKINGS

ACCESS TUNNEL
DIMENSIONS INCREASED TO 9' X 13'6"
FOR PASSAGE OF LORRIES

POWER HOUSE

EMERGENCY ESCAPE ROUTE
VIA
NORTH POLE QUARRY

OAK BLAST DOOR
(11 FEET HIGH)

CONTROL ROOM

HEATING PLANT

OAK BLAST DOOR
(9 FEET HIGH)

RECEPTION BUILDING
WITH
UNLOADING RAMP

CHAMBER NO. 5

CHAMBER NO. 2A

CHAMBER NO. 1

CHAMBER NO. 3

STEPS TO NO. 4 CHAMBER
(17" RISE)

HEATING PLANT

CHAMBER NO. 4

CHAMBER NO. 2

REAR SECTION DEMOLISHED BY
ROOF FALL, MARCH 24TH 1943.
BUILDING SUBSEQUENTLY ABANDONED
AS STORAGE AND USED AS
WORKSHOP ONLY

0   50   100   150   200   300   400   500 FEET

Having already burned its fingers over the underground project at Corsham and being completely ignorant of the dripping, fog-laden conditions underground at Manod, the Treasury balked at the prospective cost, an officer there informing Francis Rawlins that:

As to the structural costs of the scheme now in question, the item I dislike most of all is the £4,000 for 'walls'. Prima facie, the cave itself should be sufficient 'walls' as nobody proposes to actually hang the pictures. What the wall is wanted for is to provide something against which they could be leant, but it really looks as if it might be done more simply by racks or similar provision and I really do not see why they should not to a moderate extent be simply put one on top of the other.

Once the true picture had been explained to them with great patience, the Treasury finally authorized the expenditure on 4 November, but made it clear that:

…we agree to this on the understanding that the expenditure on the 'houses' and heating will be the minimum necessary to maintain a proper temperature.

Work at the quarry began immediately but was impeded by terrible winter weather and in November Temple-Richards reported that the underground repository would not be finished before February 1941. Subsequent labour difficulties involving bricklayers and carpenters further retarded progress, but it was hoped that the first of six storage chambers would be ready in April and the last by the end of May. Further delays were experienced during construction of the five-mile approach road due to the low height of a railway bridge near the village of Ffestiniog, that had a clearance of only eleven feet. The railway company agreed to lower the road level below the bridge by two feet six inches, a task that was expected to involve simply cutting away a certain amount of solid rock. They discovered, however, that the bridge was founded on compressed shale and new, deep concrete footings were required to support the bridge abutments. Nearer the quarry entrance a new access road which clung perilously to the mountainside collapsed twice during construction.

While frustratingly slow progress was being made at Manod, at Penrhyn Castle a situation was rapidly evolving that rendered the National Gallery's continued presence there untenable. On 15 April the gallery heard a rumour that the Ministry of Aircraft Production proposed to take possession of the lower floor of Penrhyn Castle including the rooms they currently occupied. Inquiries made by Sir Martin Davies revealed that following the disastrous air raid on Coventry in November 1940 it was decided that the Daimler Motor Company No.1 Shadow Factory was to be transferred to Bangor, and that the Crossville bus garage had already been requisitioned as a workshop. Daimler proposed to erect a two-storey office block on an adjacent plot but Lord Penrhyn, without prior consultation with the gallery or the Office of Works, had suggested that they use the lower floor of the Castle instead. This caused the gallery great difficulty for the annual lease agreed the previous September expired on 16 July and Lord Penrhyn was unwilling to renew as he had already agreed terms from that date with the Daimler Motor Company. When the National Gallery took up the lease it was confident that alternative underground accommodation at Manod would be available some months before expiry, but the civil engineering setbacks upset this presumption.

On 11 June Davies had no option but to inform the Daimler Motor Company, through the agency of the Ministry of Supply, that they would be unable to completely vacate Penrhyn until six weeks after the first transfer of pictures to Manod began. Davies estimated that this would be during the second week of August. He explained that the continued delay was due to the fact that the completed chambers were taking far longer to dry out than had been anticipated. Also, construction of the standby generator set was held back by shortages of material and he was unwilling to commission the quarry until the generator was properly installed and tested. Although there was a grid supply to the quarry it was unreliable and should it fail the air-conditioning equipment would stop immediately, causing irreparable damage to the pictures within a few minutes. It was unfortunate that in his explanatory letter to the Ministry of Supply Davies used the word 'inconvenient' to describe the situation the National Gallery found itself in regarding Penrhyn Castle. In reply, the MoS officer dealing with the case stated rather testily that he appreciated the gallery's difficulties but:

Then again, to us it is not so much 'inconvenience' caused as a loss of production of aero engines, which to my mind is much more important.

Manod was finally declared ready for occupation on 12 August 1941 and the first pictures were transferred later that day, the movement of all 2,000 pictures being completed by Tuesday 16 September.

The finished store consisted of five interconnected chambers approached by a three-hundred-yard heading which was originally a small drainage adit with less than six feet headroom, but was enlarged and levelled to allow access by the five-ton lorries used to transport the paintings. The natural chambers were far too large and damp to be used for storage so a series of six brick buildings were erected within the quarry, linked to one another by narrow gauge railway. The railway was extended through the access tunnel to serve a studio built on a narrow plateau outside the quarry entrance where large repairs were undertaken and the pictures viewed or photographed when necessary.

Only limited funds were available to complete the project so the underground buildings were erected with the utmost economy. The proposed buildings were not required to be heavy bomb-proof structures but they had to be absolutely dry and free from settlement;

criteria which posed something of an engineering challenge. Before construction could begin five thousand tons of rock was removed by blasting to provide the clear area required. The cavern floors consisted of loose slate debris to a depth of twenty feet, but extensive spread-footings to consolidate this loose mass could not be afforded and, in any case, there was no time for their preparation. Instead, the slate was scraped flat and then levelled with a two-inch layer of concrete upon which a continuous bitumen sheet was then laid. Brick walls with an inner compo-board cavity were erected on shallow foundations and a further concrete pad laid over the bitumen sheet, after which the loose slate chippings around the exterior of each building were drenched with a weak cement slurry applied by watering can to grout the ground. Roofs were of light compo-board tarred and covered with bitumous felt. To prevent the risk of small rock-falls penetrating the roofs, light steel mesh was laid over the felt and bonded into the brick walls.

Five of the six buildings had a headroom of ten feet while the sixth and largest was fifteen feet clear to accommodate the largest canvases. The interior of each building had a small inspection area where minor repairs such as the laying of blisters could be undertaken. Interior walls of the main storerooms were fitted with timber frames built integral with the structure to support the pictures with the need for stacking. The largest chamber served as an air-conditioned reception hall where the pictures, in their sealed transit cases, were unloaded from the lorries on a raised dock. Those assigned to other buildings were transferred in special air-tight railway wagons, the light railway system entering through curtain air locks. Although the National Gallery had acquired rights over quarry levels 'A' and 'B', the Manod Quarrying Company continued the large-scale extraction of slate from workings in close proximity to the gallery's chambers and it was thought that pressure waves from the blasting might effect the stability of the repository. To alleviate the problem as much as possible strong oak blast doors were erected in the main access passageways.

Each storage building had its own air-conditioning plant room containing electric heaters and circulating fans which enabled humidity and temperature to be closely controlled to a relative humidity of fifty-seven per cent and a temperature of 64° with a variation not exceeding 3°. Warning indicators in a central control office were activated if the temperature in any building fluctuated more than 2°. Once conditions within the quarry had stabilized the results were far better than those that obtained at Trafalgar Square before the war, and experience gained at Manod was of immense importance during the post-war period when a new air-conditioning system was developed for the London gallery. Tests carried out inside the finished chambers before the air heaters were installed indicated that under natural conditions the humidity was ninety-eight per cent at a static air temperature of 47° and mould appeared on organic material within eighteen days. During the four

The remains of two Cambridge humidity recording instruments discovered in Manod Quarry in 1986.

years of occupation by the National Gallery the air temperature in the areas of disused quarry adjacent to the storage chambers slowly increased by 5° to 52° due to heat leakage from the repositories, human occupation and heat radiated by the high wattage lamps in the access corridors. The low capacity electricity supply to the quarry could not be upgraded under wartime conditions and this proved to be the limiting factor in the design of the air-conditioning and ventilation system. The plant installed was of a simple plenum design giving four air changes per hour and was not true air-conditioning in the modern sense, in that the air was only heated, not dehumidified using a refrigeration system. Changeover between the grid supply and the quarry's standby 140 hp diesel alternator could be accomplished in two to three minutes in the event of a mains failure. A team of seven engineers on a three-shift rota maintained the plant which was subject to surprisingly few breakdowns through the war although wear was increasingly apparent by the end of the gallery's occupation.

It was known that oil and egg tempera paintings are damaged by prolonged absence of light (hence the reason why paintings hung in ill-lit corridors turn brown over time) and to counter this effect at Manod threshold lighting was maintained in the storage chambers at all times. Certain noxious gases, particularly hydrogen sulphide, also have detrimental effects upon works of art so special monitoring equipment was installed to detect these substances. Other instruments recorded the movement of air within the chambers while thermohygrographs recorded temperature and humidity.

All the pictures were transported to the quarry by lorries provided by the railway companies, the GWR being responsible for the seventy-mile journey from Aberystwyth and the LMS for the forty miles from Bangor. Standard railway containers were used for the smaller pictures and the lorries carrying these were able to drive into the quarry and unload underground at the air-conditioned loading dock. For the larger canvases the individually designed containers originally provided for the rail journey from London were reused. These were unloaded at the quarry entrance to be transported underground using three purpose-built narrow-gauge railway trucks. The trucks, one open flat wagon and two box vans with airtight bodies, were designed and constructed for the

A lorry belonging to the London Midland & Scottish Railway Company loaded with pictures from Penrhyn Castle traverses the spectacular mountain track to Manod Quarry in September 1941.

A GWR lorry loaded with pictures from the National Gallery at the entrance to Manod Quarry.

A GWR lorry laden with National Gallery pictures inside the main entrance tunnel leading to the underground repository. The brick building on the left houses the quarry's standby generator and switchroom.

Manoeuvring one of the air-tight railway wagons loaded with paintings behind storage chamber no. 3 at Manod in 1942.

A similar view taken in 1986. Railway tracks have been removed and the storage buildings stripped of their roofs, doors and all other salvageable materials.

A narrow-gauge railway container approaching the doors of storage chamber no. 3.

National Gallery by the London Midland and Scottish Railway Company at their Derby works. The fifteen-foot wagons were designed principally to carry pictures to and from the restoration studio at the tunnel mouth in seventeen-foot sealed containers. As there were no cranes available at the quarry off-loading had to be done manually, a task which took two hours for each of the larger cases and required the joint labour of the fourteen permanent National Gallery employees together with six seconded LMS platelayers. Unloading the large packing cases was made more hazardous by the high winds that were prevalent in the mountains that autumn.

Except for the big pictures, notably Van Dyck's 'Charles I On Horseback' and the large Veroneses, transhipment proceeded with little difficulty. Strict time schedules were prepared for the lorries to ensure that full and empty vehicles did not have to pass on the narrow mountain road and to avoid problems that might be caused by the fact that there was only one unloading dock underground. Three containers were moved daily on six days each week; making a total of approximately 400-500 pictures per week. The 222 pictures stored at Lord Lee's house in the Cotswolds were the last to arrive and were replaced at Old Quarries by Tate Gallery paintings transferred from Hellens and Eastington Hall.

Unloading pictures in chamber no. 6 at Manod.

Three-quarters of an inch to spare. 'King Charles I On Horseback', securely packed in its special transit case just clears the railway bridge at Blaenau en route to Manod from Penrhyn Castle. The new concrete footings for the bridge, required when the road level was lowered to accommodate the picture, are clearly visible in this photograph.

Too large for the railway loading gauge, 'Charles I On Horseback' had proved troublesome to transport from London and continued to pose problems on the journey from Penrhyn to the caves at Manod. Early on the morning of 25 September the half-ton canvas was manhandled from the large garage at Penrhyn and with great difficulty re-packed into its special, canted transit case and loaded aboard a lorry. Although the road beneath the Ffestiniog railway bridge had been lowered specifically to allow clearance for this over-sized load there was still some doubt that the lorry would pass underneath due to the sharp bend in the track on the exit side of the bridge. During the previous week three more-or-less successful rehearsals had been made with an empty transit case and on these runs the case had just scraped the apex of the bridge. Because of the bend in the road and the limited turning circle of the lorry it was necessary to lay skid plates under the bridge and force the vehicle around using jacks. On the live run it was feared that the extra half-ton load of the painting might make the lorry less manoeuvrable and the engineers were prepared to deflate the tyres of the lorry to increase clearance under the bridge. They had forgotten, however, to take into account the fact that the weight of the picture would force the vehicle down on its suspension and on the morning of the 25th it passed through relatively easily with three-quarters of an inch to spare. Nevertheless, the exercise took rather more than thirty minutes to accomplish.

Although the National Gallery took possession of the quarry towards the end of September 1941 there was much detailed work still to be done and various small contractors, overseen by the Ministry of Works, were on site for a further year. During construction the roof of the cavern in which Chamber No.2 was to be located showed signs of weakness so the design of the building was foreshortened so that no part of it would be underneath the suspect area of rock. Soon after the first pictures arrived at Manod the Ministry of Works recruited a local quarry manager and roof safety officer, Mr Vaughan, to examine the quarry and as an additional precaution the Ministry also called in the Divisional Inspector of Mines to make an independent assessment. Both men agreed that the overall structure was quite sound and further, in a private conversation, the Divisional Inspector confirmed that in his opinion Vaughan was a competent man for the job. Inspections were carried out at quarterly intervals and it was never disclosed that any problems existed, except at the point well beyond the end of the storeroom in Chamber No. 2 which had been deliberately restricted in length. There was never any indication that the roof immediately above the building posed any risk.

Despite the assurances regarding the safety of the quarry a large section of roof just beyond Chamber No. 2 fell on 9 March 1943 and rebounding boulders destroyed the end wall of the building. An

This interior view of Manod quarry shows chamber no. 2A on the left and no. 2 (the building that was partially destroyed by a roof fall in March 1943) on the right. In the background, a tunnel leads to chamber no. 1. Sections of the permanent scaffolding used to inspect the roof can be seen to the right of this picture.

immediate decision was made to evacuate pictures from the western half of the building and to reconstruct it to half its original size, but before this could be done a further roof fall the following day did substantially more damage. Due to the imminent risk of further large falls and the fact that with a wall of the building completely destroyed pictures stored there were unprotected from the quarry's harsh environment it was decided to evacuate the whole building immediately.

The National Gallery then arranged for the whole quarry to be re-inspected by a fully qualified independent mining engineer, Mr T.G. Moore, who presented his report on 22 March. It was Moore's opinion that the fall in Chamber No.2 was local in nature and that if suitable precautions were taken the building there could be safely reoccupied. Moore did not question the safety of the rest of the quarry, stating that:

> As long as the inspections by Mr Vaughan are carried out there would be no necessity of having any further opinion.

On 14 May, however, another piece of rock in Chamber No. 4 was found to be of doubtful stability and as a precaution the building underneath

Chains supporting an area of unsound roof in Manod quarry.

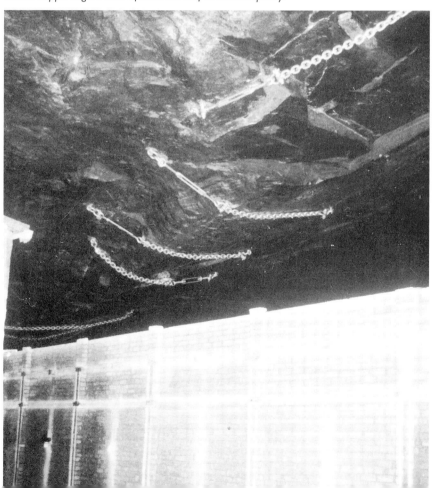

was evacuated while the suspect roof was secured with chains. Following this the Ministry of Works sent up more so-called experts to Manod, including Mr Halcrow of William Halcrow & Partners and Professor Ritson, both of whom pronounced the quarry quite safe. The National Gallery had by now lost much of its confidence in the Ministry of Works supposed expertise and demanded substantive assurances on certain aspects of safety at the quarry. Sensing that they were about to be held responsible for all the shortcomings of Manod, officers at the Ministry of Works adopted a defensive posture, effectively washing their hands of all responsibility there. A copy of an internal report prepared on 24 April 1941 by Brigadier Temple-Richards was forwarded to the National Gallery, in which Temple-Richards outlined the safety measures he had put in place at the start of the project. In it Temple-Richards recorded that:

> *Before the storage scheme was undertaken I naturally inspected all roofs to satisfy myself that these would be safe, subject to minor treatment. During the course of construction these roofs have been closely examined and inspected by me, and there were limited portions which were not deemed entirely safe. I also arranged the buildings to avoid placing them under these portions. Now that we are nearing completion and storage of valuable art treasures will take place very shortly I have had a very close examination and sounding of all roofs carried out. Where there have been small loose pieces these have been removed and I can now report that the roofs are safe against falls.*
>
> *Slate roofs require a somewhat different technique in judging them to other types of rock roofs, and in order to support my considered opinion on this matter I called in the local roof expert from the Greaves Slate Quarrying Company, a man who has 40 years experience on slate working. He has likewise examined the roofs and confirms my opinion.*

Francis Rawlins responded with a stinging criticism of the Ministry of Works that may well have remained dormant and unspoken had not the series of roof falls occurred in the spring of 1943. Rawlins accused the Ministry of Works of taking over every aspect of the planning and execution of the quarry conversion without any reference to the National Gallery's specific requirements. Rawlins went on to state that after 21 September 1941 the Ministry of Works insisted on absolute responsibility and would not allow gallery staff on site. The gallery officials felt it their responsibility to insist on certain conditions of safety for the pictures to be stored there, but the Ministry would have none of it, 'jealously guarding their responsibility for seeing how these conditions were obtained, and having resisted any attempt on the part of the officials of the Gallery to interfere in any technical matter.'

In response, the Ministry of Works reiterated the steps it had already taken to ensure the safety of the pictures but refused a request from the gallery trustees to materially strengthen the underground buildings.

Finally, Eric de Normann at the Ministry of Works issued a statement suggesting that Manod Quarry was a totally unsuitable location for the storage of art treasures, that it would not have put the site forward for recommendation had its own officers discovered it and, despite the fact that it had subsequently been investigated and approved by Mole's men in the North Wales department, the Ministry of Works disclaimed all further responsibility for:

> any disabilities which the quarry might disclose as a repository for pictures on the grounds that it was selected without any prior consultation with the Ministry.

Charged by the Ministry of Works that the National Gallery had presented them with Manod Quarry as a fait acompli, Francis Rawlins replied that that had not been the case at all and that they had merely held an option on the site until it was reported on favourably by the Ministry of Works. At this point there was a move to abandon the quarry completely but at the last moment both the Ministry and the National Gallery opted to support a recommendation by Halcrow and Ritson that a programme of constant roof inspection would ensure adequate safety. Professor Ritson also recommended that no water should be allowed to accumulate in the nearby North Pole Quarry as in his opinion the pressure of this water on the overlying strata contributed towards the roof failure. Similarly, drainage ditches were to be dug in the overlying land to prevent rain water becoming static and permeating into the quarry.

A substantial brick wall was built to support the roof immediately behind Chamber No.2, which ceased to be used for storage, remaining in use simply as a workshop. A spiders web of scaffolding and ladders was then erected in each of the caverns to enable safety men and security officers to make constant and minute inspections of the roof for the slightest signs of movement. For emergency communication within the quarry a network of twin, un-insulated copper wire was laid around all the walls and buildings, connected to a telephone in a central control room. Security guards carried portable telephones that could be clipped on to these open wires at any point.

Once these measures were put in place there were no more major catastrophes and operation of the quarry settled into a comfortable routine. Much of the day-to-day activity that was common before the war at Trafalgar Square proceeded in a similar way at Manod. Restoration and cataloguing continued and pictures were brought out to the surface studio from time to time to be photographed for publication in various journals. There was something of a reduction in the level of conservation work undertaken at Manod compared with that required in the years immediately before the war, due principally to the excellent results achieved by the air-conditioning system in the quarry. No trouble was experienced with mildew, cracking or blistering paint or warping frames. A report to the trustees prepared in January 1944 stated that:

> *Up to the time of writing the general condition of the pictures, books, drawings etc, appears to be excellent, with no sign whatsoever of deterioration due to occupation of the quarry. Scientifically, the aim in deciding upon their physical environment has been to reduce the intake and output of moisture to a minimum, and thus to diminish stresses and strains in structure as far as possible. In other words, the purpose of scientific attention is to smooth out fluctuations of relative humidity in spite of changes in voltage, barometric pressure, temperature etc. This has been largely accomplished.*

Once the existence of the Manod repository became known amongst the art collecting community, the trustees of the National Gallery were, like Sir Eric Maclagan at Westwood, inundated by requests from both institutional and private collectors begging secure storage space in their quarry. Most of these requests were looked upon favourably and by the end of the war over thirty different collections were represented at Manod, including the following:

Lord Bearstead's collection	Cambridge (Fitzwilliam collection)
Lady Bont's collection	Sir Thomas Leonard's collection
The Burrell collection	Tate Gallery (a few pictures only)
Chequers collection	Walker Art Gallery (Liverpool)
The Friete collection	Lady Cunard's collection
Gulbenkian collection	Major Anthony Blunt collection
Rothschild collection	Sir A. Beit's collection
Soane Museum	Glasgow (Hunterian) Museum
Seilern collection	H.M. The King's private collection
South London Gallery	National Portrait Gallery (part)
The Burton collection	V&A Museum (Matisse drawings)
The Bacon collection	Lady Carmichael's collection
Courtauld Institute	Hampton Court (7 paintings)
Kensington Palace	Buckingham Palace (36 paintings)
The Davies collection	Windsor Castle (24 paintings)

Among the private items stored were several rather mysterious, locked safes the contents of which were never disclosed to the National Gallery. In April 1942 the trustees inaugurated the practice of returning one picture for a short period from Manod to the Trafalgar Square gallery for public exhibition to boost the morale of the hard-pressed Londoners. At first the selected picture was exhibited for three weeks then replaced by another, but this was later changed to a monthly rotation. The nominated 'Picture of the Month' was packed into a railway container and left Manod Quarry at noon on a Tuesday, travelling via Bangor to Euston and thence to Trafalgar Square where it was scheduled to arrive the following morning. The container was immediately re-packed with the returning picture which would arrive at Manod early on Thursday afternoon. The Ministry of War Transport provided road transport from Trafalgar Square while the LMS provided a special train from Willesden Junction to Camden Town where the gallery truck was attached to a scheduled service. Guards accompanied the picture throughout its journey. By this means the number of pictures retained in London was reduced to the absolute minimum.

A hardened 'inner sanctum' was constructed within the armoured corridor in the gallery to protect the painting overnight and special arrangements were made with the LMS for a train to be kept on hand at all times so that in an emergency the 'Picture of the Month' could be returned to North Wales at two hours notice.

Plans for the return of the pictures to London were prepared in October 1944 and the first containers left Manod during Victory in Europe week. Amongst the first to go was 'Charles I on Horseback' which had caused so much trouble four years earlier. The return, however, was accomplished without a hitch; with the aid of a small crane the special container was loaded aboard its lorry in fifteen minutes and the notoriously difficult bend beneath the Ffestiniog bridge was negotiated in just twelve minutes at the first attempt.

By the Saturday following VE Day fifty of the gallery's best pictures were back on display at Trafalgar Square and by December 1945 all the pictures were back in the National Gallery after a six-year sojourn in perhaps the most astonishing treasure house in Britain.

8

THE TATE, WALLACE AND IMPERIAL WAR MUSEUM

Although, unlike the National Gallery, the Tate had not evacuated any of its pictures during the Munich Crisis of 1938, preliminary steps were taken to safeguard the collection, as recorded by the gallery's Assistant Keeper, Dr John Rothenstein, in his memoirs published soon after the war:

> *During the Munich Crisis I had considered it prudent to take down certain masterpieces and to hold them ready for instant dispatch from London, but in order to minimize public disquiet other pictures, similar in character and size, were hung in their place.*

The basement strong-rooms below the Duveen Gallery at the Tate were not ideally suited for the long-term storage of works of art and in October 1938, in view of the apparent success of the National Gallery's evacuation scheme, the trustees of the Tate Gallery decided to accept as its principal wartime retreat Hellens, an ancient, substantially built house near Much Marcle on the border of Herefordshire and

Exterior view of Hellens, near Much Marcle in Herefordshire, parts of which date from the mid-thirteenth century.

Gloucestershire, occupied by Lady Helena Gleichen, a niece of Queen Victoria. A brief survey carried out in 1938 indicated that the house was sturdy and presented only a moderate fire risk. Early the following year the gallery also earmarked Muncaster Castle in Cumberland as a secondary repository and later supplemented this with a third house, Eastington Hall in Gloucestershire.

During February 1939 preparations were made for an emergency evacuation. Arrangements were made with the Great Western and the London, Midland and Scottish Railway for six railway containers to be left in the service area of the gallery, ready for immediate packing and despatch. A schedule was then drawn up under which, on the first day of evacuation, the fifty-nine best pictures would be despatched to Hellens via Ledbury station on the GWR, and approximately 500 'B' list pictures were to go to Muncaster Castle via Euston and Barrow-in-Furness on the LMS. A small number of very large pictures including 'Death of Major Pierson' by Copley and Spencer's 'Resurrection' were too large to be easily moved and were instead walled-up where they hung. There was some argument, subsequently over-ruled, that road transport would be preferable to rail as it was probable that at the immediate outbreak of war the railway system would be swamped by panicking refugees desperate to leave the capital. It was further argued that there may not be suitable cranes to unload the railway containers at the small rural stations nearest the selected country houses, though in fact both Ledbury and Barrow had ample loading facilities.

Although details of the evacuation were kept secret from the British public, Dr Rothenstein revealed more information to a group of American and Canadian journalists shortly after the evacuation was complete. On 18 October 1939 the *Toronto Star* reported that:

More than 3,000 empty frames hang on the walls of the Tate Gallery today, says Dr Rothenstein, telling of the evacuation of the huge and priceless collection of paintings to somewhere in the English countryside.

Three days earlier, on 15 October, the *San Diego Sun* had informed its readers that:

Three hours after the Russo-German pact was initiated, the Tate Gallery took some of its greatest paintings – works by Gainsborough, Turner, Hogarth, Rubens, Whistler and Sargent – and began packing them in special crates. These works were sent to a medieval castle in a remote area of England, so situated amongst the hills that planes would have difficulty flying low over it.

On the morning of Saturday 2 September 1939 the first container arrived at Hellens where, under the supervision of Dr Rothenstein, the pictures were stacked in the Great Hall, the Dining Room and the

Drawing Room. The formidable Lady Helena greeted their arrival enthusiastically and at first looked upon the care of the paintings as her personal contribution to the war effort. She was much concerned that the fire precautions that the Office of Works were supposed to have put in place shortly after the pictures arrived had not materialized, and on 17 November she wrote to Sir Patrick Duff:

I am writing to you personally because I think you ought to know that there is no proper protection for the State Property from the Tate Gallery which is stored in my house. A man sent by the Office of Works came here before the end of August to inspect the place where the pictures were to be stored and said that fire appliances (four) were to be sent at once, the same as those supplied by the Office of Works to my rooms in St James's Palace. The 'minimaxes' [Carbon tetrachloride extinguishers] which are here in the house are expressly not to be used where there are valuable pictures. I have repeatedly applied to Mr Fincham of the Tate Gallery representing the danger should a fire break out or an incendiary bomb fall, but nothing has materialized (except a small hand spray for one bucket). I also suggested a hosepipe with a double-handled pump to get water from the pond.

Sir Patrick sent a quick, sympathetic reply promising that the required fire-fighting equipment would be dispatched that day and reassuring Lady Helena that Much Marcle was very low on the enemy target list. Five days later a much placated Lady Helena wrote to Sir Patrick:

The formidable Lady Helena Gleichen, daughter of Prince Victor Hohenlohe-Langenburg and mistress of Hellens.

Thank you very much for being so prompt. The fire appliances (two) arrived a few days after I wrote to you and now I hope all will be well. I quite agree that it is extremely unlikely that any bombs will come near here, but in such a fantastic war one never knows what to expect.

Like so many other country house owners who readily agreed before the war to make their houses available to the museums and galleries, Lady Helena was upset to find, as the first winter of war took hold, that she was having to meet the cost of the extra coal required to meet the Tate Gallery's heating requirements. By the beginning of March 1941 this had already exceeded £60, the equivalent of a year's wages for a labouring man, and gave rise to acrimonious correspondence between Lady Helena and the Office of Works. The man responsible for the Tate Gallery dispersal scheme, Dr. Rothenstein, was sent down to Much Marcle to arbitrate but was no match for Lady Helena. Reporting back to Mr Bennitt at the Office of Works on 3 March he wrote plaintively:

> *I went over to see Lady Helena Gleichen last week. I found it a little difficult to discuss the question of last year's coal bill with any force.*

The winter of 1940/41 brought home the deficiencies of all the country houses occupied by the museums and galleries. Their greatest drawbacks were that they were damp, draughty and almost impossible to heat. Even when heating was applied temperatures and humidity tended to fluctuate wildly and in some of the larger rooms the temperature variation between floor and ceiling levels could be in excess of ten degrees. In April 1941 Dr. Rothenstein arranged a meeting with Bennitt at the Office of Works to discuss the future of the Tate Gallery country houses. He explained that conditions at Hellens were particularly unsatisfactory, principally because of the unprecedentedly high heating costs, and that the largely timber-constructed Eastington Hall was too great a fire risk.

Eastington Hall, the home of Mademoiselle Montegeon, was at first considered by the Office of Works to be unsuitable for the storage of works of art, but was adopted as an emergency measure when the gallery

Eastington Hall, near Upton-upon-Severn in Worcestershire.

The smoking room at Eastington Hall, the temporary wartime home to many of the pictures from the Tate Gallery.

was damaged by enemy bombing in September 1940. Although the majority of the pictures and sculptures were evacuated before the outbreak of war, the Tate administration at first remained in London. On Thursday 19 September the Office of Works received an urgent telegram from Dr Rothenstein:

> *The gallery was damaged by a large calibre HE bomb early on Monday morning. Roof destroyed and doors and windows. Impossible to heat and work in.*

It was thought likely that the building would be struck again so the decision was taken to transfer the gallery offices and the few remaining works of art to Eastington, where they occupied the Drawing Room, the Smoking Room and the Drawing Room Corridor.

Rothenstein proposed that once the new National Gallery underground repository was commissioned at Manod, the Tate should take over the accommodation vacated at Lord Lee's house, Old Quarries, at Avening, and should also occupy parts of nearby Sudeley Castle in Gloucestershire. This scheme was agreed on 5 May but it was subsequently upset by construction problems at Manod. Two weeks later, on 17 May, Bennitt had to inform Dr Rothenstein that:

I am afraid there has been a crisis over the Manod scheme and I hardly like to give a date for the National Gallery's move from 'Old Quarries'. It is very depressing.

The Tate Gallery was finally able to vacate both Hellens and Eastington Hall on 30 July 1941, the pictures being transferred temporarily to Sudeley Castle until Old Quarries became available the following month. Eastington Hall remained empty of Crown property until October 1943 when the Science Museum occupied part of the property to store 162 crates of books from its library, previously stored at Maenan Abbey, Llanrwst. This move was necessitated by the sale of the abbey in May that year, the new owners being unwilling to continue the previous arrangements. Mademoiselle Montegeon died in November 1944 and her executors moved the remaining household to Henley Hall in Ludlow on the 15th, after which heating in Eastington Hall was shut off rendering it untenable by the Office of Works.

Sudeley Castle, near Winchcombe in Gloucestershire, was one of the houses that had not been offered to the Museums and Galleries ARP Committee before the war but was taken on by the Tate Gallery under a commercial lease in July 1941. Prior to agreeing the lease, the castle was inspected by Office of Works engineers who described it as 'a solid stone structure recently partially reconstructed and strengthened' and eminently bomb-proof. The Tate occupied the ground floor Library and Smoking Room at a rent of £120 per year plus heat and light, and was later offered further accommodation free of charge. Dr Rothenstein and three other members of the Tate staff took rooms in the tower as office space and for the storage of papers, but with the onset of winter the tower was found to be too damp and all the records had to be removed to the library in October while the staff found domestic accommodation elsewhere. Unwilling to spend another damp winter at Sudeley the administrative staff decided to return to London the following September. In May 1944, as the gallery began a rationalization of its storage capacity prior to the move back to London, it also occupied rooms in the Queen Catherine's Annexe and two first floor rooms immediately above its original allocation but these were found inadequate and given up.

Less than two months after the Tate moved into Sudeley Castle the, by now inevitable, friction arose between the Museums and Galleries organization and the service departments. At the beginning of September 1941 Dr Rothenstein was informed that a prisoner-of-war camp was to be built in the grounds of the castle, news that was greeted with alarm because nearby Tewkesbury had just been targeted by German bombers and Rothenstein feared that from the air the POW camp might look like a military establishment and attract more bombers. The Air Ministry gave reassurances that the bombing of

Tewksbury was simply a case of returning aircraft jettisoning their bombs at random, and that thus far in the war only one military camp (other than airfields) had been targeted by the Germans. Rothenstein was further assured that the prisoners-of-war posed no risk to the gallery's security, as they were Italians who had volunteered for agricultural work and would in any case be closely guarded by the military. There was little further interference until September 1943 when soldiers were temporarily camped in the castle grounds and there were rumours that they might also take over part of the building. This upset the Tate authorities, who subscribed to the widely held view that the heavy-smoking British soldier was a walking incendiary bomb. The War Office responded that this was nonsense and that far from being a fire risk the soldiers would make very adequate additional fire guards. This was all of little importance, however, as military presence was withdrawn completely on 9 December.

The Tate finally vacated Sudeley Castle on 13 September 1945, having returned the last of the pictures to London a few days earlier. Reparations required at the castle after four years of wartime occupation were minimal, amounting to just general cleaning and a little repainting of scratched woodwork at a cost of £31.

Muncaster Castle, near Ravensglass in Cumberland, the home of Sir John Ramsden, was arguably the most successful of all the dispersed wartime treasure houses. On the edge of the Cumbrian mountains, well

Muncaster Castle in Cumbria, the most remote and most satisfactory of the Tate Gallery's country house repositories.

beyond the effective range of enemy bombers and far from any worthwhile target, Muncaster Castle was largely immune from wartime troubles. The Tate Gallery occupied the three largest and most secure rooms on the ground floor of the castle, all of which were centrally heated by a modern, efficient system that consumed some thirty tons of coke through the first winter. Maintaining the best conditions for the pictures posed no problems for the staff, other than a little difficulty in securing adequate supplies of fuel during the early weeks of occupation. Fire-fighting equipment which was sorely lacking at all the other country houses had been well provided by the owner of Muncaster Castle long before the outbreak of war. Numerous fire hydrants were provided throughout the grounds and inside the castle, supplied with water from a lake many miles away high in the mountains and able to maintain a good pressure for at least two hours.

One side effect of the wartime evacuation was that many of the ancillary activities of the various museums and galleries were curtailed and among these was the Tate Gallery's public lecture programme which for many years had been organized and delivered by Mr Fagg. At the outbreak of war Fagg's services were no longer required and he found himself unemployed. In a rare moment of humanity Sir Kenneth Clark, in his role as a Tate Trustee, took up Fagg's case with the Treasury, writing:

> Regarding the position of Fagg, the lecturer at the Tate; he is un-established and is paid £265 per annum for his lectures. Needless to say these will cease and there can be no reason for paying him on that score. He is an old man of very little use in any capacity and the Tate cannot think of any way in which to employ him. On the other hand, he is almost completely destitute, and it is hard to take away his only means of subsistence. I do not know if it would be possible to give him some sort of retiring bonus from one of our funds which might tide him over until it were possible to find some modest war work for him.

In the same letter, after deviating into a discussion of other Tate Gallery matters, Clark returns to the plight of Mr Fagg:

> Since writing the above I have had another conversation with Rothenstein who says he can use Fagg as inspector or custodian of one of his dumps of pictures. I would be in favour of this because although Fagg is not very brilliant as a lecturer he is familiar with the pictures in the Gallery and could curate them adequately.

WALLACE COLLECTION

At the outbreak of war the greater part of the Wallace Collection was moved to Hall Barn in Buckinghamshire, which was the property of Lord Burnham but under the stewardship of the Lawson Estates company. To ensure safety by further dispersal a small proportion of the collection was despatched to Lady Dashwood's West Wycombe Park and to Balls Park in Hertfordshire, the home of Sir Lionel Phillips.

The detailed plans for the museum's evacuation, drawn up as early as November 1934, were finally put in motion on 23 June 1939. That evening Trenchard Cox, a gallery curator who was later to become Director of the Victoria & Albert Museum, wrote to inform J.G. Mann, one of the Directors of the Wallace Collection, that:

Owing to the gravity of the situation we have already begun today on packing the Sèvres. Foser is going to start on the majolica tomorrow. I am going through the galleries sticking a label with the catalogue number on the back of each picture. I think that all the machinery which can be set in action now is going. Certainly it looks as if we are in for trouble!

The transfer took twelve days to complete, although the bulk of the gallery's most important objects were despatched in the first two days. In total twenty-three lorry loads were despatched to Hall Barn and four to Balls Park, each truck under the charge of an assistant keeper and, according to a report by Mr J.G. Mann, accompanied by 'four able-bodied men who will travel with each lorry equipped with truncheons'. The only items to remain in London were the Marbles, Bronzes and some large tapestry furniture, all of which were taken downstairs to the specially strengthened basement bomb shelter.

While Mann took charge of things at Hall Barn the running of the Manchester Square premises fell upon another of the Directors, Francis Watson, who had hurried back to London on 28 August, cutting short a business trip to the continent. Quickly assimilating the situation, he wrote that evening to Mann, reporting that:

We have cleared quite three-quarters of the collection into the country on Home Office instructions. They rang me at home late on Wednesday night.

The following day he wrote again to Mann:

I got back from the continent last night and have found Hertford House practically empty. The staff must have worked magnificently to get so much away in five days to Hall Barn and Balls Park. The plans we had made seemed to work without a hitch and we must thank Hitler for permitting us to make the move in peace.

Watson was not the only person to express satisfaction at the progress of the evacuation. On 1 September, from his hunting lodge at Corrour in Inverness-shire where he had been kept informed of the situation by telephone, Sir John Maxwell Stirling, trustee of the collection, wrote to J.G. Mann:

To be quite honest I am not only delighted but very surprised that the move has gone so smoothly. There were so many possible snags.

There was, in fact, good reason to be pleased. Despite the urgency of the

Sunrise in a coal truck. Boucher's 'Rising of the Sun' (1753) makes a hasty departure from Manchester Square to the relative safety of Hall Barn in September 1939.

work and the delicacy of the artefacts very little damage was sustained in transit. The varnish of four paintings was slightly scuffed and vibration caused old repairs on four porcelain items to come apart, but the only fresh damage of any consequence occurred to the marble top of a French commode which was broken in two.

At Hall Barn some 474 paintings were stacked in the Large Parlour while a further nine large paintings and the gallery's entire collection of furniture found refuge in the Ballroom. A further 287 pictures were despatched to West Wycombe Park. All of the Wallace porcelain, arms and armour, miniatures and goldsmiths' work went to Balls Park, along with 147 pictures of lesser importance. The first haphazardly loaded van, bursting with pictures and its complement of truncheon wielding thugs, left Manchester Square at 2.50 pm on 24 August, arriving at Balls Park at 4.15 pm. A second van load of pictures left at 5.00 pm that day followed by a third at 6.50 pm containing armour. The following morning, Friday 25 August, the last consignment for Balls Park left Manchester Square, consisting of four cases of miniatures, four cases of porcelain, one case of goldsmiths' work and five rattling boxes of arms and armour.

For the first six months of the war the Wallace Collection shared Hall Barn with the Tower Armouries, but in May 1940 the Armouries collection was transferred to the greater security of the National

Hall Barn, the Buckinghamshire home of Lord Burnham.

Furniture and other artefacts from the Wallace Collection stacked in the ballroom at Hall Barn.

Museum of Wales leaving the Wallace in sole possession. Throughout the rest of that year sundry other items of immense value from numerous London institutions were despatched to Hall Barn, and on 11 July the contents of the museum at Richborough Roman Fort in Kent were received there. The mass of material accumulating there caused some concern to J.G. Mann with regard to the seemingly universal problem of inadequate fire precautions. Mann communicated his misgivings to Bennitt at the MoW on Boxing Day, 1940, writing that:

> *The Rubens ceiling from the Whitehall Banqueting Hall (1st instalment) arrived today. There is much valuable government property here and a trailer pump is needed.*

Just three weeks later Mann's fears were justified, for he wrote again to Bennitt on 23 January:

> *We had a small fire at Hall Barn yesterday morning. It was discovered and extinguished by the Wallace Collection staff before the arrival of the Police or Fire Brigade. Though the latter arrived quite promptly their bearing did not impress our Head Attendant very favourably, (he described them as 'proper yokels').*

Hall Barn was no more immune from military interference than most of the other country houses. In the spring of 1941 the Office of Works was informed by the Lawson Estates Company that the Air Ministry was about to requisition the Hall Barn estate in connection with Lord Beaverbrook's scheme for the concealment of aircraft by dispersal. The plan, which was applied very successfully elsewhere, was to clear an area 1,200 yards long and 200 yards wide to make a landing strip and then to camouflage it by painting hedges, trees and a small stream on the grass. Although the landing strip was to be over one mile from the house and there would be no buildings on site as the aircraft would be simply hidden amongst the trees, the museums authority was not enthusiastic. The Trustees of the Wallace Collection made personal representations to Lord Beaverbrook and in November the scheme was abandoned after a compromise plan to position the landing strip two miles from the house was rejected.

Following the death of Sir Lionel Phillips in July 1941 Balls Park was shut up and the trustees of the Wallace Collection were obliged to remove the items stored there to West Wycombe Park. This was an unfortunate but unavoidable necessity, for the heating system at West Wycombe was inadequate for the gallery's needs, but Hall Barn was, by now, bursting at the seams. Shortly afterwards the premises in Manchester Square sustained minor bomb damage and it was decided, the job of dismantling having proved easier than expected, to remove the architecturally important balustrading from the grand staircase there and shoe-horn it into Hall Barn for safe keeping.

Towards the end of the war Hall Barn again became a temporary home to items from the Royal Armouries collection previously stored in

Caernarvon Castle which, as a result of a resurgence of Welsh nationalism in the area, was becoming inappropriate for the storage of such material. Thirty containers of Royal Armouries artefacts arrived at Hall Barn in February 1944 despite the shortage of accommodation there and a further forty containers were despatched to West Wycombe Park. Meanwhile, three large wooden horses returned to the Tower of London. With victory in Europe now inevitable, the Trustees deemed it safe for the Wallace Collection offices to be reinstated in London at the end of the year, but the collection remained in Buckinghamshire until July 1945.

IMPERIAL WAR MUSEUM

Since its opening in 1920 the Imperial War Museum had accumulated a large collection of paintings and sketches of international importance, mainly by officially commissioned war artists of the First World War. Among the works held by the museum were paintings by Paul Nash, William Orpen, Stanley Spencer and John Singer Sargent and, under the general guidance of Sir Kenneth Clark, the museum's trustees were encouraged to arrange for the majority of these pictures to be sent to the country for the duration of the war.

Initially the pictures were evacuated to Colworth House at

Ramster, the country house near Chiddingfold in Surrey that housed paintings from the Imperial War Museum.

Sharnbrook, Bedfordshire, the property of Lord Melchett, and Lady Curzon's Penn House at Amersham. At Penn House the museum's largest pictures were stored in a garage because they were too big to fit through the doors to the main house. In July 1940 Lady Curzon announced that to boost her dwindling income she had found it necessary to let the house to a boys school. She expressed her hope that the garage, which was an old coach house and very large, might be partitioned in order that the Imperial War Museum might remain but this was not acceptable. An urgent search was made for alternative accommodation and in October, at the start of the school term, Mr Norman, the Imperial War Museum's overseer, reported that he had inspected Lady Curzon's House, Ramster at Chiddingfold in Surrey and found it most suitable. From Ramster he wrote:

> I will take fifty oil paintings. I want all the Sargents and Orpens in the back hall by an external door. It has a nice temperature during winter. The less interesting canvases can go in a small room opening directly outside; in case of fire they can be removed quickly. P.S: the size of the pictures does not matter, but we must keep them from damp in the winter months; heating is expensive now.

At Colworth House the pictures were stored in the Cocktail Room, the Lounge and the Ballroom, and spent a largely uneventful war untroubled by evacuees, schoolchildren or pyrotechnic soldiers. This situation was suddenly upset on 24 May 1945 when Mr Bradley, the custodian there, had to inform the Ministry of Works that due to a series of personal tragedies:

> Lady Melchett is giving up Sharnbrook; Lord Melchett is extremely ill, his elder son has been killed in action. We have to evacuate 141 pictures, drawings and sculptures – two lorry loads. The pictures at Sharnbrook are some of the most valuable. We have one month to get the pictures out.

Thankfully, hostilities ceased soon after and the pictures were able to return safely to Lambeth Road.

9

THE PUBLIC RECORD OFFICE, PROVINCIAL
GALLERIES AND ECCLESIASTICAL TREASURES

When plans were prepared for the conversion of Westwood Quarry it was expected that all the Public Record Office material previously scattered around some six or seven rural repositories would be concentrated there. This was not to be, however, and for most of the war the bulk of the PRO holding, amounting to some 2,000 tons of documents was distributed to Belvoir Castle in Leicestershire, Haddon Hall in Derbyshire, Clandon Park in Surrey, Grittleton House in Wiltshire, and the Casual Ward at Market Harborough. Small amounts were also retained in London in various tube tunnel repositories that the PRO shared with other institutions. The PRO's most historic artefacts found safer sanctuary for the duration of the war in the women's wing of Shepton Mallet prison in Somerset.

Although the prison at Shepton Mallet, one of the oldest prison buildings in Britain, had been disused since 1930 it was still retained by the Prison Commission and when, following the Munich Crisis, the Public Record Office suggested that it might make an ideal repository for its evacuated records the idea met with little enthusiasm. On 24 November 1938 Mr M. Maddaues, Secretary to the Commissioners, wrote in reply to the request of the Keeper of Records:

> *I am desired by the Prison Commissioners to say that they regret that after careful review of their probable requirements they are unable to place Shepton Mallet Prison at the disposal of the Public Record Office.*

Undeterred, however, by the Commissioners' inexplicable unwillingness to co-operate (the crime rate, and hence the prison population, having been on a steady decline throughout the 1930s resulting in the closure of numerous small and inefficient prisons), the Public Record Office, through the agency of the Office of Works, continued to lobby the prison authorities. Eventually, less than four months after their initial refusal, the Commissioners reversed their decision and, on 15 March 1939, Maddaues wrote again to the Keeper of Records:

> *In reply to your letter of the 10th instant, we shall be glad to place the women's wing at Shepton Mallet Prison at the disposal of the Office of Works for the assignment of your Office.*

Once in possession of the prison the Office of Works quickly put in place a programme to renovate the building which had fallen into a very poor state of repair during the previous eight years of disuse. Tests conducted to determine the load-bearing capacity of each cell indicated that those

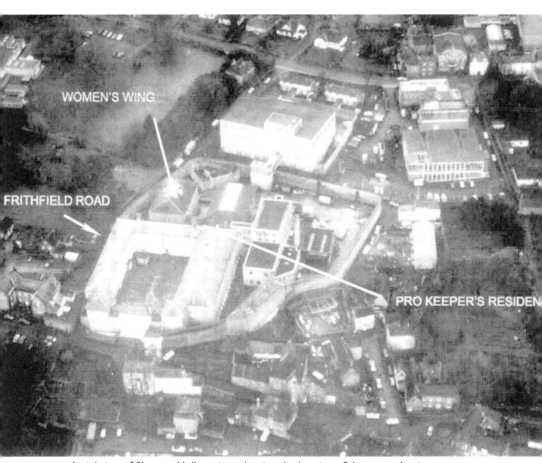

WOMEN'S WING

FRITHFIELD ROAD

PRO KEEPER'S RESIDEN

Aerial view of Shepton Mallet prison showing the location of the women's wing.

on the upper floors could support three tons each, on the middle floor four tons each and an unlimited load in the basement cells. In April plans were drawn up for the alterations required to the forty cells in the three-storey wing that was to become the PRO repository. Holes were cut in the landing floor and a dumb-waiter installed at the south end of the block to enable packing cases full of records to be moved to the upper floor with relative ease. A basement window was modified and fitted with a hatch by means of which boxes could be passed directly into the dumb-waiter from outside the building. A new coke-fired boiler and primitive heating system were installed in an attempt to ward off the worst of the damp and minimal electric lighting was installed in the main galleries. It was not, however, found practicable to install lighting in each cell so portable lamps with long trailing leads were provided instead.

A small two-storey annexe at the north end of the women's wing, at the point where it joins the main block, was refurbished to provide lodgings for the Keeper, Mr H.C. Johnson and his wife and two

Interior view of the women's wing at Shepton Mallet Prison. Note the lift installed by the Public Record Office at the right-hand rear of the building and the absence of wire netting between floors, which was removed to enable items stored in the prison to be evacuated quickly in the event of fire.

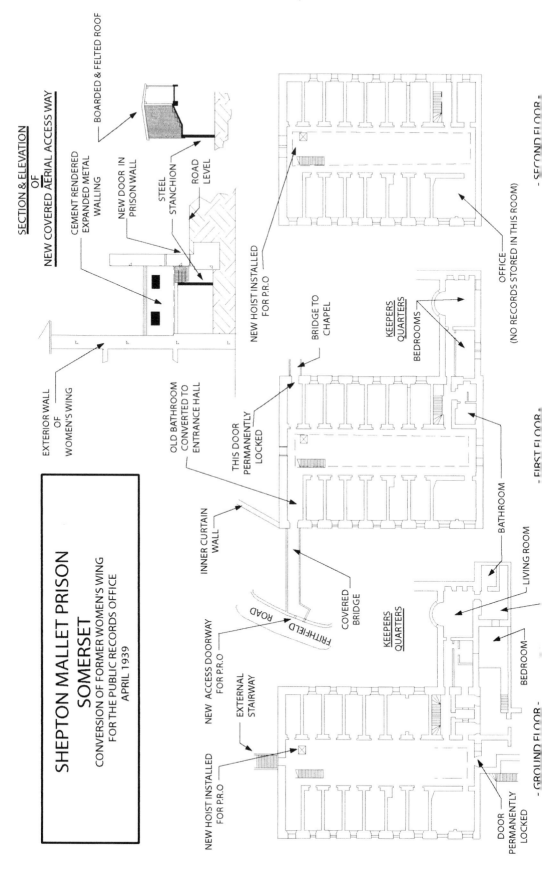

SECTION & ELEVATION OF NEW COVERED AERIAL ACCESS WAY

BOARDED & FELTED ROOF

CEMENT RENDERED EXPANDED METAL WALLING

NEW DOOR IN PRISON WALL

STEEL STANCHION

ROAD LEVEL

EXTERIOR WALL OF WOMEN'S WING

SHEPTON MALLET PRISON SOMERSET
CONVERSION OF FORMER WOMEN'S WING FOR THE PUBLIC RECORDS OFFICE
APRIL 1939

NEW HOIST INSTALLED FOR P.R.O

BRIDGE TO CHAPEL

OLD BATHROOM CONVERTED TO ENTRANCE HALL

THIS DOOR PERMANENTLY LOCKED

KEEPERS QUARTERS

BEDROOMS

OFFICE
(NO RECORDS STORED IN THIS ROOM)

- SECOND FLOOR -

INNER CURTAIN WALL

COVERED BRIDGE

FRITHFIELD ROAD

KEEPERS QUARTERS

BATHROOM

- FIRST FLOOR -

LIVING ROOM

NEW ACCESS DOORWAY FOR P.R.O

EXTERNAL STAIRWAY

NEW HOIST INSTALLED FOR P.R.O

KEEPERS QUARTERS

BEDROOM

DOOR PERMANENTLY LOCKED

- GROUND FLOOR -

children. This work was completed during September and Johnson and his family moved in at the end of the month. Commenting on the accommodation, he later wrote:

We found great difficulty in negotiating our furniture through the very narrow prison doorways but my wife, David and Elizabeth have accepted very well their new and unusual environment, in fact the children enjoy it.

Shortly after the first consignments of records arrived from London on 22 August 1939 it was decided that a separate, secure and enclosed entrance to the PRO repository should be built and that the repository would then be sealed off from the rest of the prison, which had by that time been earmarked for use by the War Office. A new opening, protected by a security door, was made in the outer curtain wall of the prison adjoining Frithfield Road. Because the prison was built in a horizontal clearing in an otherwise steeply sloping hillside the ground level of the prison yard was some eight feet lower than Frithfield Road, necessitating the construction of an eighteen-foot-long concrete bridge to span the gap between the curtain wall and the first floor of the women's wing. An old bathroom on this floor had a large hole knocked through its exterior wall for use as an entrance hall.

With preparations at the prison now complete a constant stream of lorries arrived from London at the rate of between one and three each day until the end of November, by which time approximately 300 tons of documents had been delivered, packed in 10,000 uniform cardboard boxes. Shepton Mallet prison was the wartime home to the most important, iconic documents in the PRO collection including the Magna Carta, the Great and Little Domesday Books, the Death Warrant of King Charles I, the log books of HMS *Victory* and, with no little irony, Chamberlain's pathetic piece of paper promising 'peace in our time'.

The PRO's tenure at Shepton Mallet was under intermittent threat from the military authorities during the mid-war years. Occupation of the remaining sections of the prison by the War Office as a Military Detention Barracks under the command of Colonel Fraser in October 1939 caused no immediate problems, but in May 1941, after another military detention centre in Hull sustained severe damage from enemy bombing, pressure was put on the PRO to relinquish its section to the War Office. This was successfully opposed, as was a similar representation by the United States Army, whose 2912 Disciplinary Training Centre took possession of the detention barracks in October 1942. United States servicemen found guilty of serious offences from the whole European theatre of war were detained at Shepton Mallet. During the four years of US occupation a special red-brick execution room, incongruous against the grey limestone of the old prison walls, was erected by the US authorities and there twenty-three inmates convicted of capital offences were hanged. Two others of American

Cell No. 10 at Shepton Mallet Prison stacked with documents from the Public Record Office.

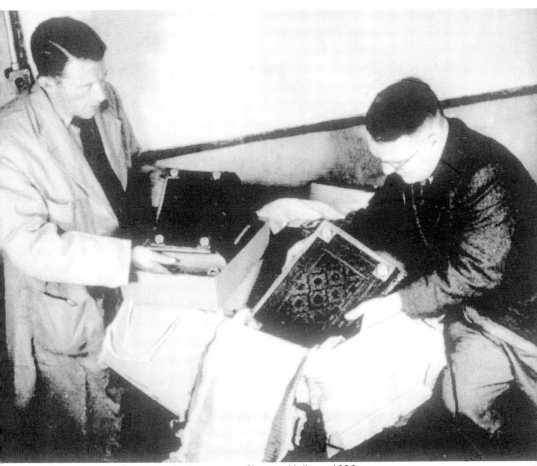
Great and Little Domesday Books arrive at Shepton Mallet in 1939.

Indian extraction, privates Benjamin Pygate and Alex Miranda, were executed by firing squad in respect of their religious beliefs. No special provisions were made for these shootings and that of private Miranda went horribly wrong. The condemned man was simply stood against the prison wall to meet his death and the bullets of the execution party ricocheted back from the hard stone, seriously injuring several members of the ten-man firing squad.

The American presence proved beneficial to the Public Record Office in an unexpected manner. Because of the vast number of service records the Disciplinary Training Centre was required to process it was provided by the US authorities with a Graflex microfilm camera, a technology virtually unknown at that time in the United Kingdom. Johnson, the PRO's man at Shepton Mallet, was quick to appreciate the value of this equipment and successfully persuaded the Americans to allow him to take microfilm copies of many of the records in temporary storage in the prison. This was the beginnings of the PRO microfilm library. Lord Bath, at Longleat House, got to know of the American microfilm equipment and subsequently arranged for many of the Longleat manuscripts to be duplicated.

There was a moment of panic in the summer of 1942 as the war seemed to encroach upon the hitherto peaceful Mendip hills. The City of Bath had sustained terrible damage over two successive nights in April, and on 29 June a mass attack upon the seaside town of Weston-Super-Mare destroyed many buildings and killed 102 of its inhabitants. It was reluctantly decided that to further safeguard the collection some of the items of lesser importance should be distributed elsewhere and on 5 July, with the aid of a small Royal Engineers detachment, several lorry-loads were evacuated to Grittleton House in Wiltshire.

In July 1945, with the war drawing to a close, the Public Record Office, like all the other great London institutions, was anxious to return to normality as soon as possible. The return began on 10 July and reached its peak of intensity in January 1946, much of the loading onto lorries being undertaken by German prisoners-of-war from camps on the Mendips. Great Domesday, however, travelled back to London anonymously and unguarded under the personal charge of Sir David Evans, in a large briefcase on the front passenger seat of his private motor car.

Material from smaller London institutions and the provincial museums was also despatched to the relative safety of remote country locations. Furniture and Marbles from the Soane Museum were sent to the Tenants Hall at Rhianva in Anglesey, while the collection of architectural drawings by Flaxman, Chantrey and Robert Adam spent the war years in the cellars of Haig Hall near Wigan. For the first fifteen months of the war the contents of the Geological Museum remained in Kensington under conditions of dubious security, but during a four week period over New Year 1940/41 the bulk of the collection was transferred to the University of Wales at Bangor. The entire contents of the Natural History Museum, meanwhile, was dispersed to over twenty country houses including How Capel Court in Herefordshire, Tattershall Castle in Lincolnshire and Fort Rodborough near Stroud in Gloucestershire. The museum's 'Type Specimens' were secreted in Carthouse Quarry at Godstone in Surrey, a former firestone quarry that had latterly been used as a mushroom farm. After rough conversion for secure storage at the start of the war the quarry was used jointly to store the Natural History Museum's specimens and a large, privately owned collection of vintage wines.

Both the Walker Art Gallery in Liverpool and the Manchester Art Gallery initiated rolling public exhibitions of many of their modern paintings after 1941. This scheme took its inspiration from an earlier project initiated by the Tate Gallery and organized by the Art and Entertainment Emergency Council to distribute its collection of modern works. Commenting upon this scheme on 18 April 1940 the *Daily Sketch* reported that:

The first fruits of its plans were shown today at the Tate Gallery in the form of a collection of modern pictures organized by the Contemporary Arts Society. This exhibition is to be shown to the public first of all in the Victoria Art Gallery in Bath, which will be opened by Sir Kenneth Clark on May 4th. At the same time examples of modern lithography will be shown at the Bath School of Art and at village schools and halls in the district.

These enlightened schemes served a dual purpose; the safety of the paintings was enhanced by very wide distribution and, by exhibiting the pictures at such places as factory canteens and army camps art was brought to the masses from whom such things had previously been socially excluded. The Walker Art Gallery's thirteenth to sixteenth century paintings were sent for safe keeping to Knowsley Hall, Croxteth Hall, Rufford Old Hall and Ellesmere College, but its extensive collection of modern pictures by the likes of Wilson Steer, Sargent and Algernon Newton were sorted into groups of thirty and circulated around selected public schools. Those establishments participating in the scheme included Rossall, Sedbergh, Giggleswick, Repton, Shrewsbury, Denstone, Merchant Taylors, Howells' at Denbigh and the Rydal School in Conway. The distribution of Manchester's collection was more egalitarian, the pictures being exhibited at local art galleries, schools, service camps, works hostels and factory canteens throughout Lancashire and the north of England. Some of the more notable modern paintings by Walter Sickert, Augustus John and William Rothenstein were put on permanent exhibition in Buxton, while the gallery's world famous collection of Pre-Raphaelites was put in charge of the National Gallery at Aberystwyth and eventually transferred to Manod.

Ensuring the safety of the historic treasures from the great London churches and provincial Cathedrals was amongst the most difficult problems to overcome because many of the finest artefacts were architectural features that were integral parts of the buildings they adorned. Just before the war the Bishop of London, Dr Fisher, formed a committee to oversee the protection of such artefacts from London's churches, while responsibility for the many other ecclesiastical buildings throughout the country devolved upon the Central Council for the Care of Churches. Many of the finest examples of timber reredoses, screens, pulpits, churchwarden's pews and complete organs were removed bodily and transferred to the safety of the West Country, the majority eventually finding their way to Westwood Quarry. The Horesman and Byzantine textiles from Durham Cathedral were also transferred to Westwood along with church plate and medieval stained glass from scores of lesser churches. In Bristol a stained glass window, reputedly a gift from Nell Gwyn, was deposited in a nearby cellar while other Bristol treasures were stored in disused tunnels on the long abandoned Hotwells Railway.

Most of the priceless artefacts from St Paul's Cathedral, including the wrought iron screens, the Grindling Gibbons carvings from the choir and Sir Christopher Wren's model of the Cathedral remained within the Cathedral building, buried deep in the immensely strong crypt which was specially air-conditioned for the purpose.

Throughout the country church bells, like the sixteenth century peal from St Bartholomew-the-Less of 1510 and the six bells from St Andrew Undercroft, were removed to the country for safe keeping, while elsewhere bells were lowered from their towers as a safety precaution.

10

CONCLUSION

Sir Kenneth Clark was anxious to see all the National Gallery pictures returned to Trafalgar Square as quickly as possible after VE day and by Christmas 1945 this task had been successfully accomplished. Some pictures from the private collections stored at Manod, however, remained incarcerated there for several years, often for reasons of great tragedy. The owners of a number of these pictures lost their lives during the Blitz and the ponderous mill of British civil law was slow to

Cases of sketches and watercolours leaving Westwood quarry en route for London in 1945.

Taken in 1945, this photograph shows crates of V&A artefacts being removed from the quarry for return to Kensington.

determine the rightful inheritors and in the meantime the paintings remained in subterranean limbo.

The first of the V&A items to return to Kensington from Westwood Quarry were the notebooks of Leonardo da Vinci, which were despatched on 6 June 1945. Thereafter there was a lull until March 1946 when several lorry loads of material were packed for departure and the full programme of repatriation began. Further batches were returned in May, July and October 1946, followed by a final consignment, including

Towards the end of 1945 museum artefacts were gradually returned to London. Here we see cases of V&A material about to leave, while on the right-hand side of the corridor can be seen the first of many thousands of ex-War Office Royal Enfield motorcycles which were returned to the underground factory at Westwood at the end of hostilities to be rebuilt, re-sprayed and sold as new.

the larger items of furniture and architectural artefacts, which left Wiltshire on 1 March 1947.

British Museum exhibits stored at Westwood were removed over a similar time frame, but those artefacts which found refuge in the London tubes, including the Elgin Marbles and the heavy Assyrian statuary, remained in storage until the winter of 1948/9. Evacuation of artefacts from Aldwych began on 7 December 1948 and continued on every Tuesday through December and the following January. The Elgin Marbles departed as ingloriously as they had arrived, by late night ballast train to the LPTB Lillie Bridge yard and from there to Bloomsbury by lorry under cover of darkness. British Museum material and the Buckingham Palace chinaware stored in the disused sections of Piccadilly station were returned to their respective homes in April 1948, but the collection of Tate Gallery statuary remained until 4 November 1949 when, under pressure from the LPTB, it was transferred into temporary storage in Brixton until the Tate Gallery was ready to receive it.

Immediately after the war, as the pictures and other priceless artefacts

141

This modern photograph shows that little has changed at Westwood since 1945. The museum repository was taken over by Wansdyke Security in 1985 and stone extraction resumed in other sections of the quarry shortly afterwards. Cut blocks can be seen stacked in the former car parking area to the left.

drifted back to their respective museums and galleries it was questioned whether the massive upheaval involved in the evacuation had been worthwhile. The answer was unequivocally 'yes'. Although the damage was less severe elsewhere, the Tate Gallery, the British Museum and the National Gallery all suffered considerable damage. Bombs completely destroyed one exhibition hall at the National Gallery and many doors and roof lights elsewhere in the building were smashed. Had the contents not been evacuated earlier the loss would have been incalculable.

Despite all the careful planning and preparation there were still significant losses. The only important picture lost from a London gallery was the Tate's 'Destruction of the Children of Niobe' by Richard Wilson, painted in 1760. This was destroyed by fire when a private workshop in St James's, to which it had been sent for restoration before the war, was bombed during the Blitz. Many of the smaller artefacts from the V&A that were not despatched to Montacute or Westwood for safe keeping were widely distributed among the provincial museums, many such having been on loan since before the war. The majority survived unscathed, but an important collection of Sheffield plate, loaned to the Sheffield School of Art was ruined during an air raid on the city. When Bristol City Museum was badly damaged by bombs in November 1941 a fabulous collection of Bow and Chelsea pottery on loan from the V&A was destroyed together with an extensive collection of 18th Century century glass.

PREPARATIONS FOR THE NEXT WAR

Immediately after VE day consideration was given to the long-term future of the two permanent repositories at Manod and Westwood. The Trustees of the National Gallery at first advised caution, suggesting to the Ministry of Works and Building in October 1945 that maintenance should be kept up at Manod 'in case the need should arise again'. Over the next eighteen months, however, the euphoria of peace, despite the growing unease in Berlin, forced thoughts of future war into the background and by January 1947 the MOWB was urging the National Gallery to give up its tenure of Manod Quarry as the maintenance the gallery insisted upon was costing £4,600 each year, which the Ministry thought was money thrown away to no good.

No immediate decision was made but within a few months events developed in Europe that were to cast a malign shadow over the civilized world for the next fifty years and force all western governments to the realization that the untidy end of the Second World War was not going to ensure perpetual peace thereafter. With the threat of atomic war upon the horizon, the National Gallery Trustees sought the advice of Sir Wallace Akers, the former Chief Technical Advisor to the government on atomic energy who had been deeply involved in the 'Tube Alloys' project, Britain's wartime atomic weapons programme. Akers reported that the quarry offered ideal protection against radiation and strongly advised that it should be retained. Meanwhile the Cabinet Office had initiated preliminary surveys of certain of the Corsham quarries and determined that they too offered excellent protection. It was decided that Westwood would be retained as an art treasures repository, and the much larger Spring Quarry site in Corsham was, in 1956, selected as the location of the Central Government Emergency War Headquarters. Maintenance of the Westwood site posed no problems as the larger part of the quarry remained in use as a Ministry of Supply factory and shared many of its services. A new, Crossley-engined diesel alternator was installed during the late 1950s to replace the unserviceable Lister-Petter set that had caused so much trouble through the war years, but the original air-conditioning and heating equipment was retained.

During the autumn of 1950 international tension had again increased to the point where one false diplomatic move might trigger atomic war. In October a refurbishment programme was implemented at Manod, a new generator and sub-station was installed and plans again prepared for the mass evacuation of works of art from the London galleries. Agreement was also reached to accommodate 150 pictures from the Royal Collection at Manod. Requests were also received from many other private art collectors, including one from Count Seilern on behalf of Prince von Liechtenstein which was politely refused on the grounds that there would probably be insufficient room to spare. Towards the end of October a practice evacuation involving some 200 pictures was undertaken, principally to test the transport organization put in place by the recently nationalized British Railways. Further rehearsals took place intermittently and with decreasing frequency throughout the 1950s and 1960s.

Meanwhile, there was a resurgence of interest in the tube tunnels that had been pressed into use during the war. In October 1950 the Tate Gallery approached the London Transport Executive with a query regarding which of Aldwych and Piccadilly the Executive considered the safest and most bomb-proof structure. The Tate was surprised to be informed by Miss O.E. Crockett that the Home Office was already interested in both properties, had done scientific investigations there and had 'determined that both could be perforated by no more than a conventional 500 lb bomb.'

During the war a ring of flood gates had been put in place that would close across the tunnels on the lines most vulnerable to flooding should the Thames embankment be breached or major sewers be damaged by bombing, effectively sealing those sections off from the rest of the underground system. The wartime flood gates were not considered to be an adequate solution and as a feature of the government's post-war nuclear home-defence planning a second, outer ring of flood gates was proposed. In her report on the viability of Aldwych and Piccadilly as shelters in an atomic war, Miss Crockett continued:

Both stations are below flood level of the river and the London Transport Executive are considering the question of duplicating the main Tube flood gates by new gates outside the area in which the two stations considered are situated. If the present flood gates fail or are by-passed the two areas under consideration would be within the drowned area.

Home Office interest in the tubes caused some consternation at the Tate Gallery. The gallery along with the other major London institutions until this time looked upon these places as their own emergency boltholes, reserved for them simply by virtue of their previous occupation, should atomic war start with a 'bolt-from-the-blue' as American paranoia would have it, and before a full-scale evacuation to Wales could be put in play. An internal memorandum dated 15 December 1950 noted plaintively that:

It appears that the Home Office have already asked for a survey of London Underground accommodation for public shelter purposes.

Full details of this survey have never been disclosed but it must have revealed a surfeit of suitable accommodation because, on 26 January 1951, the Tate and the British Museum were informed that the two tube stations were once again earmarked for their use. The little information that is revealed of the Home Office survey indicates that the tube stations were allocated to one of four categories:

i. Above flood level
ii. Below flood level but protected by two sets of flood gates
iii. Below flood level but protected by one set of flood gates (the wartime gates re-engineered)
iv. Below flood level and not protected by flood gates

Categories (i) and (ii) were considered atom bomb proof, category (iii) was considered proof against high explosive bombs, and category (iv) as vulnerable to all forms of attack. The most pertinent point of this categorization is that, in the early 1950s, parts of central London were still considered viable for both humans and art treasures, even under attack from atomic bombs.

By the summer of the following year the Tate Gallery had unilaterally decided that the accommodation offered at Piccadilly was no longer adequate and gave up all future claim to it the following December. The British Museum, meanwhile, had maintained, through the agency of the Ministry of Works and Building, a lease on the Aldwych repository that was due to expire in 1959. In March 1955 Aldwych was still one quarter full of British Museum artefacts awaiting return to Bloomsbury, and the museum now requested permission from the MOWB to use the rest of the space there as a general store for all sorts of non-perishable and unimportant materials including such things as packing cases and moulds used for reproductions and repairs. The MOWB response was:

We certainly make it a rule that emergency storage accommodation shall be kept empty so as to be available at a moment's notice in case of need, but I am not sure that we shall be as strict in applying this rule to tube shelters as we are to the prepared quarries.

The 'prepared quarries' (Manod and Westwood) were kept under strict MOWB control. A new twenty-one-year lease was agreed for Manod in September 1958, but when this expired in 1979 no one seemed to notice and the Department of Education, upon whom responsibility had devolved, continued to squat there for a further three years. Similarly, the lease on Westwood was extended until 1985 but then allowed to lapse. The complex air-conditioning system there had been run continuously in anticipation of a sudden emergency until July 1978.

The most salient feature of the early- to mid-1950s plans for the evacuation of art treasures, should Britain become embroiled in an atomic war, was that they were in all essential details identical to those prepared for the conventional weaponry of the Second World War. Basing their conclusions upon the effects of the atom bombs dropped on Hiroshima and Nagasaki, defence analysts believed that the immediate aftermath of atomic bombardment of British cities would be similar to the aftermath of large-scale conventional bombardment. More people were killed and more buildings were destroyed in Tokyo, they argued, in one conventional bombing raid than in Hiroshima by the atomic bomb. Because the effects were much the same except on a larger scale, the remedies would be the same also, and it was for this reason that the already anachronistic Civil Defence Corps was allowed to survive for another decade or more. In 1950 it was not even automatically assumed that the Third World War would necessarily be an atomic conflict. There was, however, one axiomatic assumption and that was that whatever form the conflict took there would be an adequate warning period, allowing time to organize the evacuation or shelter of the civil population and time, as in 1939, to pack up all the nation's treasures and despatch them to remote corners of the Kingdom.

It was not until 1958, when American intelligence revealed that the USSR had the capability to launch inter-continental ballistic missiles carrying nuclear (as opposed to atomic) warheads against targets anywhere in the world, that the impotence of existing plans was made clear to all. Launched by missiles, nuclear warheads with yields 1,000 times greater than the atomic bombs that struck Japan would reach their targets in minutes, literally 'bolts-from-the-blue', and lay absolute waste to whole cities in a flash. There would be no warning and no time for phased evacuation. In reaction to these circumstances a new plan was developed for safeguarding at least some of the treasures. The plan was codenamed Operation Methodical and was fully developed by late 1962, just in time to miss the Cuban Missile Crisis. 'Methodical' was in most respects little different from what went before. The pictures and other treasures would still go to Manod and Westwood and, as in 1939, they would travel by night, but they would go by road rather than rail. Road transport allowed flexibility, so alternate routes and venues were prepared. If bombs on Birmingham, Liverpool or Chester made North Wales unviable the twelve-vehicle convoy would divert to Gloucestershire where once again the country houses, or what was left of them, would play host again.

A key feature of 'Methodical' was that, because of the anticipated absence of warning, only a relatively small number of the best, most iconic pictures and other artefacts were earmarked for evacuation. The majority of the pictures, like the majority of the civil population, would be abandoned to fend for themselves. A further feature of the plan, committed to the record in 1962 but kept secret for thirty years, was that even if there was a warning period before the bombs fell or the missiles struck, the national treasures would still remain in London until the very last moment. Similarly, Central Government would decamp to their long-prepared bunker in north Wiltshire just hours before the anticipated onslaught. The rationale in both cases was the same: to act earlier would indicate that Government had given up all hope of peace and would destabilize the civil population, causing panic, revolt and anarchy.

Between 1979 and 1982 Home Defence planning for nuclear war underwent a radical restructuring. Central government peremptorily dumped virtually all responsibility for individual survival or the continuity of the nation's cultural institutions, concentrating their limited assets and abilities instead solely upon the prosecution of war and measures to ensure the 'continuity of government' in the American style. An extensive, underground infrastructure created during the Second World War, much of it disused for two decades but retained as an insurance against future conflict, was suddenly disposed of. Among

The gutted remains of storage building no. 4 at Manod in 1986.

The entrance to Manod Quarry in 1986.

these disposals were the arts repositories at Manod and Westwood. By 1985 Manod was in private hands, used first as a set for the acclaimed cult BBC drama 'Edge of Darkness' and then the following year for a surreal advertisement for BMW motor cars. When visited by the author in 1986 the site was in a sorry state. Most of the metalwork had been removed for scrap and anything else of use, roofing timbers, doors, light fittings, railway track etc, had been removed leaving just the empty brick shells of the storage sheds. In recent years increased quarrying activity has swept away all but a short length of the entrance tunnel at Manod. Westwood Quarry reverted to its pre-war owners, the Bath and Portland Stone firm, and in 1985 its subsidiary company, Wansdyke Security, adapted it at minimal cost for use as a high security commercial document store. Following a management buy-out in the 1990s the same function continues there today.

INDEX